COMBAT KICK BOXING

Pat O'Keeffe

CHIEF INSTRUCTOR MOD-KA KICK BOXING

CHIEF INSTRUCTOR MOD-KA KARATE-JUTSU

HEAD AND BRITISH TEAM COACH (K.I.C.K.)

SUMMERSDALE

Summersdale Publishers Ltd
46 West Street
Chichester
West Sussex
PO19 1RP
United Kingdom

www.summersdale.com

Printed and bound in Great Britain.

ISBN 1 84024 195 0

Acknowledgements

Special thanks to Glen Sweeney for the photography, ideas and professionalism, and to my wife Cathy for the additional camera work and tolerance in the face of some bizarre scheduling!

Also, grateful thanks for the patience and friendship of the cast of villains portrayed by the following martial artists:

Jim McAllister   – Kick boxer and 4th Dan karate
John King   – Ex-kick boxer and 5th Dan Go So kempo
Chris Keeliher   – Kick boxer and 3rd Dan karate jutsu
Barry Gardiner   – Kick boxer and 1st Dan karate jutsu
Rob Panther   – Kick boxer and karate-ka
Tony Wakeling   – Karate-ka
Phil Thomson   – 2nd Dan karate-ka

About The Author

Pat O'Keeffe's first encounter with kick boxing was in the mid-seventies when as a private student he studied a blend of Goju Ryu karate and kick boxing under the legendary Steve Morris for some two years. Prior to this he had trained in karate, judo, ju-jitsu and aikido and currently holds a 4th dan in Mod-Ka karate-jutsu.

In April 1979 he met and started training under Geoff Britton, the then British B.A.F.C.A. team coach, and remained his student until 1989 when Geoff moved to Spain.

Whilst with Geoff Britton, Pat had twenty-eight kick boxing fights starting in October 1979 and finishing in October 1987. During this fighting career he fought three World Champions and the Belgian professional champion, Rudi Van Damme, a fight that appeared on *World of Sport*, the only time that kick boxing has been shown in a sports programme on terrestrial television.

Towards the end of his career he fought Nigel Benn the W.B.C. ex-World Professional Boxing Champion who was competing in both kick boxing and boxing at that time.

Since then Pat has officiated as both a judge and referee at every level in the sport including international events and has appeared on Meridian Television.

Now a successful trainer, he is presently the British head and team coach for the American kick boxing organisation K.I.C.K.

Contents

Preface

The worldwide explosion of martial arts from the mid-sixties to the present day is a social phenomenon that bears some examination. Kung fu, karate and kick boxing are three martial arts that enjoy broad recognition amongst the general public, mainly due to films and television.

Many other martial arts, some quite esoteric, are gaining a significant profile. Quite why these ancient fighting systems are in vogue in the early twenty-first century is at once both complex and simple to explain.

There are some very good reasons for studying martial arts, among them are health, fitness and recreation. Given the amount of time spent on leisure in the last twenty years in particular, it is not so surprising that martial systems offering more than just a work-out are attractive.

But the heart of matter is surely the deep psychological need for physical confidence in an age when, despite all the technological advances made by man, society persists in being violent.

For the public at large, martial arts mean self-defence. They are not always sure just what the numerous systems are, or their relevance to physical protection, but they generally accept that there exists a body of knowledge and skill that can enhance their chances of successfully defending themselves in the event of being attacked.

It doesn't help when so many differing styles and systems are on offer. What is the difference between karate and kung fu? Is silat the answer, or should I seek out capoeira? Added to these traditional systems are many modern adaptations that combine or 'surf' various elements from different styles.

Unfortunately, just to really confuse the picture, we as human beings frequently have our own agendas when looking into the business of self-protection. Some people, because they espouse a pacifist viewpoint, are drawn to so-called 'soft' martial arts such as tai chi chuan or aikido, irrespective of whether such systems can provide the necessary elements of a realistic self-protection system. This approach can be summarised as: 'I couldn't possibly hurt another human being, so I'm learning a non-aggressive form of self-defence!'

Others see the so-called 'hard' styles, such as karate or tae kwon do as the answer, but many of the hard styles are tied into ways of training that simply don't 'cut it' when it comes to modern-day violence. The words 'tradition' and 'respect' often mask an instructor's lack of real fighting capability, though many of their adherents would have a purple fit if you suggested that. To their minds, sweating and hundreds of basics equal street effectiveness.

The truth is that the answer to realistic self-defence is far more elusive than picking a martial art at random and training twice a week for a few months or even a few years, because so many of the martial systems offered to the public are no longer truly martial (warlike) in nature. They have been altered and toned down, so as to attract and keep students.

Of the two approaches though, my own feeling is that a hard system has more going for it – you should be fitter when it comes to running away!

It is inevitable that with this ever-expanding catalogue of martial arts there has been a parallel explosion of martial arts books and therefore, by implication, self-defence books. Here the subject is just as problematic.

Books on self-defence range from the illusory to the realistically graphic. Whilst many show simplistic defences against stereotypical attacks with little, if any, hard information on how, why, where or when, there are also books of genuine worth out there, but they can be very hard to identify.

The good books usually have an author with a proven background in **applied martial arts**, whose skill and knowledge has been hard-won and then distilled in harsh post-attack reflection, before being taken back into the arena and applied. Or they come from an era when the emphasis was on martial art not martial sport.

Whilst it is hard to recommend martial arts' styles or clubs suitable for realistic self-defence, there are books that can be recommended. I have included in the back of this book an A-list of what I have found to be solid texts on this vital subject. I have given each a mini-review. Hopefully the reader will be interested enough to seek out some, if not all of these books.

Having asked searching questions of other styles and books, what is there to recommend this one?

It has to be said from the beginning that this book is not exhaustive on the subject of self-defence. No book, regardless of dust jacket claims, can be. What it sets out to do is bring a kick boxing perspective to the attention of the serious self-defence student. It asks him or her to consider the techniques of kick boxing as a viable basis for self-defence and the kick boxer as an example of a survivor.

Many people reading this book will not be kick boxers (ring fighters) or even necessarily training in kick boxing. They will read this book because of the lurking suspicion in every martial artist's mind that what happens inside the kick boxing ring is very close to the real thing; that the skill, strength, stamina and sheer guts of kick boxers are a solid base on which to build realistic self-defence.

By the late seventies I had trained in many martial arts styles, some hard, some not so hard. My time under Steve Morris, from 1974 to 1976, was my first introduction to kick boxing. The training was a Goju karate/kick boxing mix that produced a fierce fighting style. The Earlham Street dojo was not a place for faint hearts.

It left me however with a taste for full-contact fighting. I felt then, as I still do now, that it teaches technique under pressure or, to put it another way, how to get hurt and still function competently.

In 1979 I met Geoff Britton, a gifted kick boxing instructor with a lateral approach to training and fighting. I stayed with Geoff until he moved to Spain in the late eighties. His analytical approach to contact fighting changed the type of martial artist I was to the extent that I still quote him to students and in my books.

Between Geoff Britton and Steve Morris I believe I had a privileged schooling in the harsh world of kick boxing – the yin and the yang. I have also had to deal with what can best be described as 'situations' and these did nothing if not reinforce the harsh lessons I have learnt along the way.

If you are serious about self-defence I believe you have to experience the shock – and I mean *shock* – of getting hit. For then you must find the **strength of will**, for that is what it is, to overcome the opposition.

It is not being esoteric or deliberately obscure to say that you are fifty per cent your own opposition: your fear, your lack of composure, your lack of fitness, your unawareness, your lack of technique, will defeat you as surely as the assailant who attacks you. Unless you are mentally prepared to be hurt, battle through and overcome assailants, you will be beaten and probably, in today's world, very badly.

This book will only provide some of the answers, no more, no less, for after reading it, you must practise and at some stage that means full contact; harsh, but true. If you do practise then some bruises are inevitable, but the experience is invaluable.

There is an old martial arts saying that is often repeated, but it bears saying again for the simple truth of it:

'The iron thinks itself pointlessly tortured in the furnace and
beaten on the anvil – the sword look back and knows why.'

Foreword

It is a great pleasure for me to write the foreword to this new book by Pat O'Keeffe, not least because its subject matter – self-protection – is one that is close to my heart. Most people seem to broach the subject of self-protection via books, videos and classes, in a totally unrealistic manner. They cram page upon page, frame upon frame and speech upon speech with unrealistic and totally unworkable physical techniques that would have you falling at the first hurdle in your bid to protect yourself or those that you love. This book is refreshingly different; it is far more comprehensive and contemporary, it prepares people for reality with honesty and integrity. We need books of this quality if we are going to stay safe on the volatile streets, and equally we need gutsy authors and instructors like Pat who have the wherewithal to take life-saving information and convert it into readable and legible ink.

This marvellous book covers everything you might need to avoid, escape or survive a real attack, from the all important awareness, which allows you to avoid conflict before it even begins, to vital targets, to the very controversial, but imperative pre-emptive strike. The inclusion of the latter – the pre-emptive strike – is impressive. Why? Because Pat is one of the very few people in the martial arts' world brave enough to get off the fence and underline its validity in real combat. I know of many credible martial artists who will privately admit the importance of striking first when your life is threatened, but only the smallest minority have the courage of their convictions to place their views in print.

There is a massive responsibility when you write a book on personal protection, because if you are not honest with people and do not tell them how it is, warts and all, then you fail to prepare them, or even worse you ill-prepare them, and that could cost them their life. Pat has shouldered that responsibility admirably; he has stepped up to the plate with courage and I commend him for that. I highly recommend this book because it tells it how it really is. Please read it and get your kids to read it; the information might be all you need to escape serious attack, or even death.

Geoff Thompson
Coventry 2002

Introduction

Kick boxing has many aspects that recommend it as a *core* for a self-defence system. It has simple, streamlined techniques that can be absorbed quickly and training drills that emphasise 'feedback', such as focus pad and bag training.

Further, the hard conditioning work-outs serve to enhance strength, speed and stamina beyond that of most martial arts, but ultimately, what sets kick boxing apart from so many martial systems is **contact sparring**, that unblinking judge of all skill that tears away theory and cant. You might look the world in the eye and tell it that you are a superb fighter with the answer to every situation, but you can't lie to your body.

The problem with choosing kick boxing is that it is a sport. It has rules and a structure that make it unrealistic and artificial as far as self-defence is concerned. There are no gloves in the street, no rounds, no referee to ensure fair play, and contact sparring, hard and testing though it is, is only one-on-one.

Therefore the first task to make kick boxing suitable for self-defence is to remove the rules. This means that other techniques, but more importantly, other targets, are now available. Approximately 70 per cent of this book is sport kick boxing techniques and targets. The other 30 per cent is made up of techniques expressly forbidden in the ring.

Ultimately, what recommends kick boxing is the *product*: the kick boxers themselves. When properly trained, a kick boxer is a hard, superbly conditioned individual with fast, powerful techniques that have been honed to the point where attack and counter-attack are seamlessly joined; an individual who has chosen to exist in an arena where the lessons have been hammered home.

In summary, to convert sport to combat kick boxing, we must keep the *product*, but remove the rules.

In the first book in this series, *Kick Boxing – A Framework for Success*, the requirements to succeed in the sport of kick boxing were set out, examined and defined with the aim of producing a capable exponent of a martial sport. In this book we shall take the techniques of the sport and adapt them for the street, adding new skills and re-examining old ones in the process. Ideally this book should be read after *Kick Boxing – A Framework for Success*.

Although this book is aimed at the practising kick boxer, it is relevant to any person practising a pugilistic martial art, providing that they come with an open mind and a willingness to learn. The man in the street devoid any of martial arts training is strongly recommended to seek out a good kick boxing or Thai boxing club to thoroughly ground him in the basic skills.

Chapter One
Awareness – The Beginning and the End

When man was a hunter-gatherer, he was in tune with the world in which he lived. He knew that danger lurked in many forms and he used his intelligence and wits to devise skills that would keep him alive.

Modern man has constantly sought to bring that wild environment under control to the extent that there is little true wilderness left. With the rise of cities and law and order, people have passed on the responsibility for their safety to a variety of civil servants and institutions: policemen, soldiers, doctors, nurses and safety experts. People live in various artificial environments where danger in any form is reduced to a minimum.

As a result, most people feel more or less safe and spend their lives 'switched off', reacting to circumstances rather than anticipating them. Such people are potential victims.

There are many examples in everyday life: traffic accident victims who did not look or listen before crossing the road; sailors and hikers who ventured out without reading a weather forecast or having emergency equipment; fire victims who did not extinguish cigarettes or who overloaded electrical sockets; customers who used hole-in-the-wall cashpoints without being aware of what was going on around them. The list is endless, but there is a common thread – they failed to be aware.

In terms of self-defence man did not realise that when he created his safe environment he brought with him the most dangerous animal in the wilderness – himself.

Martial artists do not generally see themselves as victims, yet that very attitude can blinker them. It must be remembered that physical skills cannot be used unless the threat is perceived early, its potential danger is assessed, and evasion, whenever possible, is employed.

In the ring, fighters are brought to the middle, touch gloves and are instructed to come out fighting. In the street, you can be attacked from all sides simultaneously with no prior warning.

Awareness is the first rule of self-defence; without it physical skill is redundant. Awareness, like any other skill, must be practised and maintained. To assist with developing awareness, practising the colour coding system is recommended. Be aware of your state of mind.

Colour Coding

White: Switched Off.

This is the everyday frame of mind that most people inhabit. Switched off, unaware, distracted, call it what you will, it might just as easily be called victim mode.

Yellow: Switched On.

This is the frame of mind you might be in when crossing a busy road. You are not frightened, but you are aware of the potential danger and you naturally switch on by looking and listening. Incidentally, most mothers with young children are continually in 'Yellow' state.

Orange: Specific Threat.

This is where you are personally involved. You might be in 'White' state talking to friends in a pub when suddenly you hear an argument at the other end of the bar. Your awareness increases – you have just switched to 'Yellow' state. Now one of the people arguing notices you looking and says, 'What the ★★★★ are you looking at?' You are specifically threatened and have just switched to 'Orange' state.

Red: It's Happening!

You are being attacked. Most victims of crime go from 'White' state to 'Red' in one swift, pain-filled, bewildering moment. However, many situations escalate slowly and the more aware you are, the greater chance you have of avoiding them and leaving the area.

Predators in the wild are always on the lookout for the old, sick, young, isolated and the unaware. Equally, the modern city predator uses the same markers. In a study in America criminals were asked to view a film of an ordinary street full of people and pick out their likely targets. Although these criminals were tested separately, they repeatedly picked out the same individuals.

In the area where I live a new modus operandi has been developed that is proving very profitable for teams of muggers.

One gang member will scout for the group by watching for customers using credit cards or large sums of money. He or she will pick their moment to move in and mark the clothing of the potential victim with chalk, usually around the shoulder area.

The main gang will be waiting down the street. When a chalk-marked person passes them, they will follow, pick their spot and attack, knowing that their victim has profit potential.

There are many variations on this theme, but they all boil down to the same pattern: the mugger has weighed your ability to defend yourself, assessed the profit potential and picked an ambush point that affords a clear advantage. Given that muggers often outnumber their victim and are usually armed, the odds are clearly stacked in their favour.

Yet if you are switched on, careful not to flash credit cards or money around, and look and walk confidently, you reduce your chances of being a victim considerably.

Awareness is the key

I'm not suggesting that you become paranoid, I'm saying that you should get into good habits. Your attitude should be that of someone crossing a very busy road, switched on, looking and listening, but not afraid.

Chapter Two
Targets and Techniques

Most offensive techniques of sport kick boxing are immediately transferable to combat kick boxing, giving trained kick boxers their *core techniques*. However, because there are no limits to targeting in the street, all the so-called 'illegal' areas of sport kick boxing – the throat, kidneys, lower abdomen, calf, groin and so on – are available to be attacked.

Standard sport combinations such as left hook to the body/left hook to the jaw can become truly devastating when 'street-adapted', to left hook to the groin/left hook to the throat. Likewise, jab/cross to the head followed by a roundhouse to the head can be transformed into jab/cross to the head followed by a roundhouse to the groin, thigh or calf.

The appendix has a number of diagrams showing all the target areas referred to in this book, and specific diagrams are included in this chapter for the sake of clarity.

The speed, power and fluidity of sport kick boxing combined with streetsmart targeting is a sound basis for combat.

Stance and Guard

Ring fighters are constantly taught the value of good stance and guard. In gyms you will hear coaches calling out, 'Keep your chin down,' or 'Keep your elbows close to the body,' and the infamous, 'Don't cross your feet!'

In street situations, particularly when you are the victim of an attack, you will rarely, if ever, have time to adopt a proper stance and guard; therefore all techniques and combinations must be practised from 'natural' positions. However, once in a dangerous situation you must protect yourself with a realistic guard. Failure to do so will see you quickly taken out of the action. In the case of a gang attack a tight guard and nimble footwork may be *all* that you are able to attempt in terms of realistic defence.

Attacks sometimes arise out of steadily escalating situations, such as overheated arguments. In these circumstances there are covert stances and guards that you can adopt without making the other person more angry or alarmed. Further, your position in relation to your potential assailant or assailants and the environment that you find yourself in – for example, back to the wall or back to a staircase – will undoubtedly affect the outcome.

Cross Arm-Ready Stance

In figures 1 to 4 we see an argument in progress. As the larger man becomes more aggressive, the smaller man performs a series of small changes to the way he stands.

1) He turns slightly, so that his body is angled away, thereby reducing the target options of the other man. (Fig. 1)
2) He crosses his arms, so that they are in a position to either strike or block. (Fig. 2)
3) He drops his chin slightly so that it is not open to a fast knockout punch. (Fig. 3)

4) He ensures that his feet are a shoulder-width apart and his weight is spread fifty-fifty on each foot so that he can move swiftly in any direction. (Fig. 4)

As you adopt the **cross arm-ready stance** you should quickly become aware of your environment. Is the other person alone? Are you exposed on any or all sides? What is your potential escape route?

Fig 1

Fig 2

Fig 3

Fig 4

Thinking Man Stance

In figure 5 we see a similar body and foot position to the cross arm-ready stance, but with the difference that the right hand is held on the chin. This is added protection against a blow to the face and also leaves the hand in position to launch a strong right hand counter should it prove necessary.

Either of these stances will assist in preventing you getting caught by a sucker punch. It has to be borne in mind however that the nearer you are to your potential assailant, the easier it is for him to strike you before you can react. A covert guard and good distance appreciation will increase your chances.

Fig 5

Fighting Stances and Guards

Once the action starts you are advised to go quickly into a fighting guard. There are three fighting guards:

1) Full Guard

An aggressive guard that enables you to deliver fast punches and kicks. (Fig. 6)

2) Cross Guard

A defensive guard used to cover up under a heavy assault. It is accompanied by a rapid up and down bobbing motion. Strong hooks can be thrown from this guard. (Fig. 7)

3) Half Guard

A guard used primarily in close fighting. It limits the offensive options of your assailant. (Fig. 8)

For fuller explanations of these three guards see *Kick Boxing - A Framework for Success*, 'Chapter One – Fundamentals'.

No guard or stance by itself can fully protect you. They have to be supplemented by movement, parrying and blocking. However, they will protect your upper body and reduce the target choice of your assailant.

It should also be borne in mind that what protects you from a kick or punch does not necessarily protect you from being grabbed or wrestled to the floor.

Fig 6

Fig 7

Fig 8

Offensive Techniques

The offensive techniques in the kick boxing arsenal translate to combat with little, if any, modification. However, as stated in the introduction, many more targets come on-line in combat and a well-trained jab to the throat or a right roundhouse kick to the groin has a genuine man-stopping ability that is easy to appreciate.

The Jab

In the context of self-defence, the jab is an explosive stop/hit. That is, a lead hand punch thrown the second your assailant moves. Its aim is to stop your assailant or jolt him or her out of their stride. The arm is kept loose until the very last instant when it is stiffened and driven through the target area. (Figs. 9 and 10)

Fig 9

The right hand and arm must come up to protect you at the same time the jab is thrown. The right hand guards the jaw and the right elbow is kept tight against the ribs.

The four essentials for an effective jab (figure 11) are:
1) Keep your chin down.
2) Your right arm guards your jaw and ribs.
3) Your left shoulder touches your cheek.
4) Look along your left arm like a gun sight.

There are many targets for the stop/hit, though the eye, chin and throat are the most effective. It is unlikely that the jab will be sufficient on its own to finish your assailant's attack, but with practice it will stun your assailant long enough for you to either

Fig 10

Fig 11

follow up with other techniques or escape.

The best tool for sharpening the jab is the focus pad and the best drill is the 'snap up' focus pad drill. Have your partner hold the focus pad against their chest, then, at varying intervals, he or she 'snaps up' the pad and you respond by throwing the jab as fast and hard as you can. (Figs. 12 and 13)

This practice method will work your reflex speed, limb speed and body speed. (See *Kick Boxing – A Framework for Success*, 'Chapter Seven – Speed and Power'.)

The bag should be used to gain raw power. Throw three sets of ten jabs, ensuring you 'sink' the punch as far as you can into the bag. (Fig. 14)

Practice can be made more varied by starting from different positions, for example with your hands down at your sides, from the cross arm-ready stance or the thinking man stance. Further, you should also practise throwing double jabs as this is the fastest of the stop/hit combinations and can finish the fight before it begins.

Fig 12

Fig 13

Fig 14

The Cross

The cross is a straight-arm punch delivered with the rear hand to a range of targets on both the body and the head. It is a very powerful blow capable of ending a fight on its own, particularly when it hits the target accurately.

My army sergeant summarised the difference between a jab and a cross thus:

'The jab is the can-opener and the cross is the spoon that digs the meat out.'

I used this quote in the first book of this series and I make no apologies for using it again, so succinctly does it describe the role of each of these punches.

To throw the cross, rotate your body quickly towards your assailant and throw your right hand, keeping your chin down. Your rear foot advances half a pace to place your body weight behind the punch. Your left arm comes up to guard the left side of your head and body. (Figs. 15 and 16)

There are a number of variations on the cross and you should refer to *Kick Boxing – A Framework for Success*, Chapter One, for a more complete explanation. Use a combination of 'snap up' focus pad drills and the bag to turn this punch into the big decider that it should be.

The best target options for a cross are the chin, jaw, throat, temple and eye on the head, and the solar plexus, liver, lower abdomen and kidneys on the body.

Fig 15

Fig 16

Fig 17

Fig 18

The Hook

The hook is a curved punch of infinite variety that is meant to come around an assailant's guard. Although it can be used at long, middle and short ranges, it is primarily a short-range punch.

To throw a hook, pivot strongly with your ankle, hip and shoulder, letting your arm leave your chin at the last possible moment, thus making it hard for your assailant to read it. Keep your elbow high and finish with your chin tucked well down. (Figs. 17 and 18)

In street situations you are spoilt for choice with this punch when it comes to targets. On the head, the jaw, chin, temple, eye and throat are all targets. Targets on the body include the solar plexus, liver, floating ribs, lower abdomen and the kidneys.

When used as a counter I believe the hook to be without equal. The nature of the punch is that it curves outside of your assailant's line of vision, making it very hard to read. The degree of 'hook' can be controlled very accurately, making it extremely versatile. You should experiment to find your own preferences, using a combination of focus pad drills and the bag.

A full range of hooks is described in the first volume of this series, *Kick Boxing – A Framework for Success*. There is one variation on the hook that is particularly effective and warrants description here.

The Shovel Hook

The shovel hook is a punch halfway between a hook and an uppercut. It is thrown in the same way as a hook except the angle of attack is 45 degrees. It is essential to pivot explosively as you throw the punch. (Figs. 19 and 20)

There are four main targets for the shovel hook, all on the body. They are the solar plexus, liver, lower abdomen, and the kidneys.

Punches to the body will slow down an assailant and in many cases finish the fight there and then. An unconditioned body hit by an accurate shovel hook will crumple and fold. Remember, in the street you have the option to hit 'below the belt' and there is no finer weapon for this than the shovel hook. Spend equal amounts of time on both the focus pads for accuracy and the bag for power.

Fig 19

Fig 20

Fig 21

Fig 22

The Uppercut

The uppercut is a short-range punch meant to come under or between the guard of your assailant. It utilises a strong pivot of the ankle, hip and shoulder and because of this it is best thought of as a vertical hook.

From a tight guard, pivot at the ankle, hip and shoulder, taking care not to telegraph your intention by throwing the punch in a loop. Keep your arm close to your body and only release it at the last second. Your forearm should be at a 90-degree angle to your upper arm on contact. (Figs. 21 and 22)

The main targets for this punch all fall on the centre line of the body. These are the chin, solar plexus and lower abdomen. Again, you should use the focus pads for speed and accuracy and the bag for power.

There are two additional pieces of equipment that assist in building strong hooks and uppercuts: the 'angle bag' and the maize ball. (Figs. 23 and 24)

These two pieces of equipment enable you to throw hooks and uppercuts through more angles than is possible with the normal bag and so practise the maximum number of angles of attack.

Both hooks and uppercuts are best thrown in combination when the one sets up the other. Because the path of each of these punches is circular, it is important to curve the body behind them to achieve maximum power.

Fig 23

Fig 24

The Elbow Strike

The elbow strike is arguably the strongest of the arm blows. It is a close-range strike that has great versatility with many angles of attack and therefore many potential targets.

You should spend a great deal of time mastering this superb weapon. Experiment with focus pads and the bag learning the different types of power – whip, spin, snap and thrust – that compliment each strike.

It must also be borne in mind that the elbow has three striking surfaces, the front edge, back edge and point. (Diagram 1)

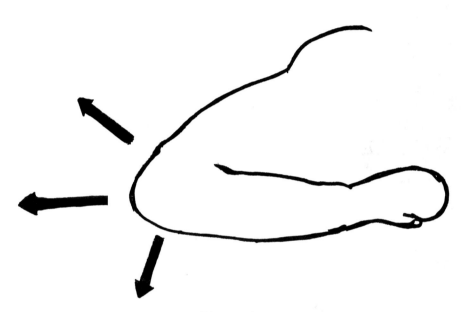

Diagram 1

Forward Elbow Strike

Striking Surface: Point

To throw the forward elbow strike, snap your elbow sharply forward in an arc and strike the target with the point. (Figs. 25 and 26)

The main target for this strike is the solar plexus. This strike can be utilised at very close range and can also be used to set up either a short cross or whipping elbow.

Fig 25

Fig 26

Fig 27

Roundhouse Elbow Strike

Striking Surface: Front edge

To throw the roundhouse elbow strike, pivot quickly and whip your elbow round in a circular path, striking the target with the front edge. (Figs. 27 and 28)

It is very important to keep in mind the idea of whipping the elbow through with maximum speed, curving the body behind the blow.

There are many target areas for the roundhouse elbow strike. These include the temple, jaw, throat, solar plexus, liver, floating ribs and the kidneys.

Fig 28

Side Elbow Strike

Striking Surface: Point

The side elbow strike is used primarily to attack assailants to your left and right. You can attack assailants to the front by utilising a body turn during a combination.

To throw the side elbow strike, thrust the point of your elbow directly to the side, generating power from the shoulder. (Fig. 29)

If space permits, you can increase the impact by taking a sidestep towards your assailant and co-ordinating the movement so that you hit your opponent as you land, thus placing the maximum body weight behind the strike.

The target areas for the side elbow strike are the eye, throat, solar plexus, ribs, lower abdomen and the kidneys.

Fig 29

Back Elbow Strike

Striking Surface: Back edge and point

The back elbow strike is used to counter an attack from behind. For this reason it is well-suited to breaking holds. (See Chapter Three.)

To strike, clench your fist and thrust backward with the point or rear edge of your elbow, using the shoulder to generate power. (Fig. 30)

Extra power can be added by twisting at the waist.

The main targets for the back elbow strike are the jaw, throat, solar plexus and the lower abdomen.

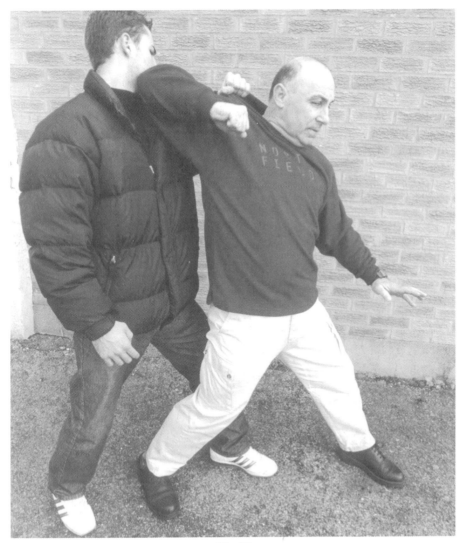

Fig 30

Descending Elbow Strike

Striking Surface: Point

This is *the* finishing blow. It concentrates the full force of your body weight downward on to the point so that the power is driven into the target area.

To execute this strike, raise your elbow upward and then drive it down, sinking your hips as you do so. (Fig. 31)

Additional power can be obtained by jumping up prior to dropping your weight. The descending elbow strike is especially useful when breaking holds. It can be driven downward into the wrist or forearm of your assailant to free yourself. (See Chapter Three.)

The main targets for this strike are the nape of the neck, the collar bone, between the shoulder blades and the kidneys.

Fig 31

Rising Elbow Strike

Striking Surface: Front edge and point

A useful close-range weapon that performs a similar function to the uppercut. The rising elbow strike creates great power within a short distance.

To throw the rising elbow strike, thrust the elbow upward in a tight arc, curving your body to add power. (Fig. 32)

The main targets for the rising elbow strike are the chin, solar plexus and between the shoulder blades.

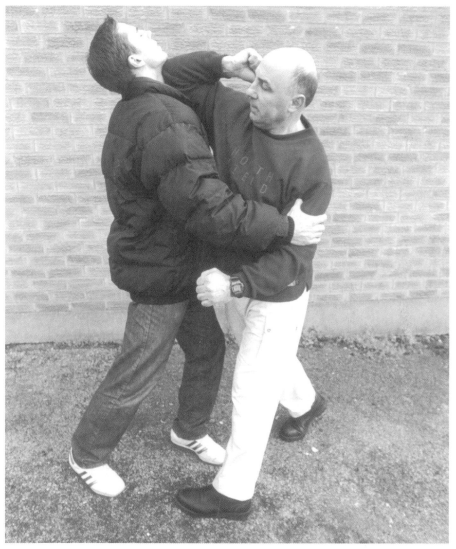

Fig 32

Whipping Elbow Strike

Striking Surface: Front edge

This strike is very powerful and deceptive in that it utilises a fast downward whipping motion, curving the body behind it. Its origins lie in Thai boxing where its use has been perfected.

To throw the whipping elbow, rotate your body to the left and bring your right arm over, striking your assailant's temple. The strike describes an almost vertical arc. (Figs. 33 and 34)

Use the focus pad held at an upward angle of 45 degrees to practise this strike.

The main targets are all on the head: the temple, cheek bone, jaw and the bridge of the nose.

Fig 33

Fig 34

Spinning Elbow Strike

Striking Surface: Back edge and point

The fastest of all the elbow strikes, the spinning elbow also generates great power by having the entire body spinning behind it. It works best as part of a combination or as a powerful hold-breaker.

To throw the spinning elbow strike, quickly turn 180 degrees and drive your elbow around in an arc. Like all spinning techniques, it is essential to turn your head and body ahead of the elbow. (Figs. 35 and 36)

There are many targets for this strike, but a useful aid is to remember that many of them lie on the centre line of the head and body: between the eyes, under the nose, the chin, throat, sternum, solar plexus and the lower abdomen are all targets.

Additional targets not on the centre line are the nape of the neck, the heart, liver, kidneys and between the shoulder blades.

Fig 35

The elbow strikes are almost a mini-fighting system in themselves, so great is their range and adaptability. In close-range combat mastery of the elbow along with the other 'natural' weapons – the knee, head and heels – will go a long way to deciding the outcome.

Fig 36

Kicking

The legs are the most powerful weapons available to the fighter. They are longer and stronger than the arms and with practice also become faster. Kicks should be thrown to the body and legs because they are bigger targets and are not as mobile as the head.

In the ring the experienced kick boxer can afford to throw head kicks because the rules do not allow grabbing or throwing. In the street however you will be grabbed, kicked in the groin and thrown to the ground (possibly all at once!) if you attempt to throw high kicks, especially 'cold' high kicks.

There are always exceptions to rules and the exceptions are:
1) When you have used an effective lower level kick to set up the high kick.
2) When your assailant has been weakened and his guard is down.
3) When you are an exceptional kicker.

To remove all doubt should any still remain, I strongly recommend that you only use high kicks not when *one* of these conditions prevail, but when they *all* do. The floating ribs and the kidneys, on approximately the same line, are the highest targets at which you should normally aim. Remember, the penalties for getting it wrong are severe and possibly permanent.

The Knee

So obvious is the knee's use as a weapon that even untrained street fighters will readily use it to the groin and head, but it is only with training that this 'natural' short-range weapon reaches its full potential.

The three methods of attack are:
1) The forward knee kick
2) The roundhouse knee kick
3) The rising knee kick

The target areas best suited to the different kinds of knee kick are shown alongside the respective explanations of how to execute them. One target area deserves a special mention – the leg. (Diagram 2)

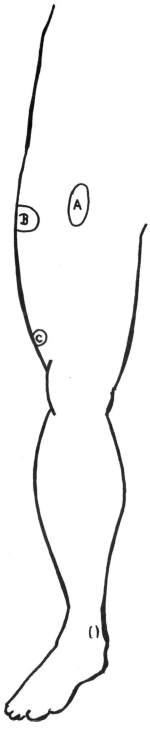

Diagram 2

Knee kicks to the front of the thigh, common peroneal nerve, and the muscle insertion point above the knee, serve a number of functions:

1) They will incapacitate your assailant by sending his muscles into severe spasms, making it impossible for him to fight effectively, chase you, or even stand up.
2) The pain is a severe deterrent. I have seen tough, seasoned Thai boxers sitting on the floor weeping from the pain of leg kicks.
3) The leg is a non-lethal area and can be hit very hard without the fear that your assailant will suffer permanent injury or death. As such they are near perfect for self-defence.

All kicks should be worked on the bag for power, the shield for mobility and the focus pads for accuracy.

Fig 37

Forward Knee Kick

To throw the forward knee kick, bend your knee and drive it forward with a strong hip action. Aim to go *through* the target, rather than just striking the surface. (Figs. 37 and 38)

The main targets for the forward knee kick are the stomach, lower abdomen, the front of the thigh, the common peroneal nerve and the muscle insertion point above the knee.

Fig 38

Roundhouse Knee Kick

The roundhouse knee kick is a circular kick that is ideally suited to striking the targets on the outside of the leg and it combines very effectively with the roundhouse kick. (See figure 46 – low-level roundhouse kick.)

To throw the roundhouse knee kick, bend your knee and raise your leg to the side. Pivot on your supporting leg and bring your knee around in a circular path to strike your chosen target. (Figs. 39 to 40)

The main targets for the roundhouse knee kick are the floating ribs, lower abdomen, the muscle insertion point above the knee, and the common peroneal nerve.

Fig 39

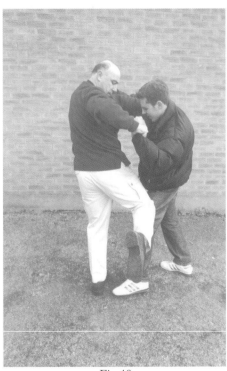

Fig 40

Rising Knee Kick

The rising knee kick could be considered the ultimate uppercut. When it is combined with seizing and pulling down your assailant's head, thereby unbalancing and setting them up, it is devastating. (Fig. 41)

To throw the rising knee kick, raise your knee rapidly upwards and strike the target, thrusting your hip behind the action to increase its power.

Many of the targets for the rising knee kick are on the centre line of the body. Further, because the head can be seized and drawn down (see figure 41) it can also be considered a viable target.

The jumping version of the rising knee kick is a very strong ring technique, but its use in the street is too big a gamble. It is never a good idea to have both feet off the ground, because landing makes you extremely vulnerable to having your feet kicked from under you.

Lastly, the very nature of the rising knee kick makes it an efficient hold-breaker.

The main targets on the front of the head and body are the facial area, chin, sternum, solar plexus, liver, floating ribs, lower abdomen and groin.

The main targets on the rear of the body are between the shoulder blades, the small of the back and the coccyx.

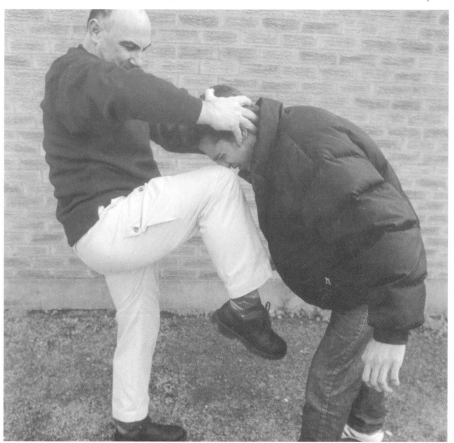

Fig 41

Lead Leg Front Kick

The lead leg front kick is a fast jolting kick that causes little disturbance to your balance and guard. It readily combines with other kicks and punches and is the easiest of the kicks to time, thus making it an effective stop/hit. The stop/hit version of this kick is called the defensive lead leg front kick.

To throw the defensive lead leg front kick, bend your knee and point it at the target you have chosen. Snap the leg straight and drive your hip in behind the kick to add power. Make contact with the ball of your foot. (Figs. 42 and 43) Use the 'snap up' focus pad drill to sharpen your stop/hit timing.

The other version of this kick is the attacking lead leg front kick.

Fig 42

To throw this version, bring your rear leg up and place it behind the front leg. Bend the knee of your front leg, pointing it at your chosen target, and snap the leg straight. Because your body weight is moving in behind this kick, it is stronger than the defensive version.

The main targets for the lead leg front kick are the stomach, lower abdomen and the knee. It is important to remember that *all* kicks should be withdrawn immediately after making contact, otherwise your leg will be grabbed.

Fig 43

Rear Roundhouse Kicks

The rear roundhouse kick is found in all variations of kick boxing because of the tremendous power that can be attained with it. Low, middle, high and jumping variations all occur in the ring, but here we will concern ourselves only with the low and middle-level kicks.

Although superficially the low and middle variations are thrown in the same way, the low-level roundhouse kick is of particular importance in terms of self-defence and will be dealt with separately.

Middle-Level Rear Roundhouse Kick

To throw the middle-level rear roundhouse kick, pick up your rear leg with the knee tucked to the side. Pivot sharply on the support leg and drive your hip forward. At the same time snap your knee straight. Make contact with either the instep or the shin. (Figs. 44 and 45)

Fig 44

It is important to emphasise the three factors which combine to give this kick its power. They are:

Fig 45

1) The fast pivot on the support leg, thereby making the body power the leg. Too many people throw this kick without concentrating on the pivot, allowing the kicking leg to *pull* the body around with it.
2) The hip preceding the kick. This action ensures a greater commitment of body weight into the kick.
3) The knee snap.

All three factors are necessary for the kick to reach its full potential. Work the kick on the bag until it has real power, make the bag fold around the leg. Then add the shield for mobility and finally, the 'snap up' pad drills for accuracy and speed.

In *Kick Boxing – A Framework for Success* a number of variations on the middle-level rear roundhouse are shown. These variations produce differing effects, such as increased speed or increased power and so have self-defence implications that are worth researching.

Targets for the middle-level rear roundhouse kick are the groin, lower abdomen, stomach, floating ribs and the kidneys.

Fig 46

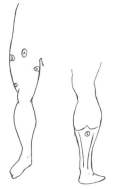

Diagram 3

Fig 47

Fig 48

Low-Level Rear Roundhouse Kick

The low-level rear roundhouse kick originates in the indigenous fighting art of Thai boxing, where its effectiveness has been proven in the ring time and time again. This powerful and extremely painful kick can totally incapacitate an assailant whilst at no time placing their life in danger.

To throw the low-level rear roundhouse kick, pick your knee up slightly and drive your hip forward, pivoting on the support leg at the same time. Snap the knee straight, making contact with the shin. (Fig. 46)

It is very important not to look down at your opponent's leg as this telegraphs the kick. Maintain a tight guard throughout the kicking action.

The main target areas for this kick are the lower calf, common peroneal nerve, the muscle insertion point above the knee, and the inside of the thigh. (Diagram 3)

When used to hit the common peroneal nerve, a variation of this kick calls for a pushing action with the shinbone on contact. It adds to the effect and is perhaps the most painful and incapacitating of the leg kicks.

A truly knockout combination can be made by throwing a low roundhouse to either the common peroneal nerve, or the muscle insertion point above the knee, and then immediately following it with a roundhouse knee kick to the same target. (Figs. 47 and 48) Practise this on the six-foot bag until it becomes second nature – it is a genuine man-stopper.

Warning: Whenever you throw low-level kicks remember to keep your hands up.

Lead Leg Roundhouse Kick

There is a significant difference between the sporting and combat versions of this kick. In the ring the knee is picked up before pivoting into the delivery, but for the street it is a faster and more deceptive technique when thrown straight from the floor. In combat, the lead leg roundhouse kick is used mainly to attack the groin in a fast snapping motion.

To throw it, lunge forward off your rear leg and snap your leg straight, curving it into the target. (Fig. 49)

Use the 'snap up' focus pad drill to achieve a fast, accurate kick.

Fig 49

Lead Leg Side Kick

The lead leg side kick can be used as both a stop/hit and as a punishing finisher. Like the lead leg front kick, there are two versions of this kick, the attacking and the defensive. Further, the very nature of this kick makes it especially suitable against weapon attacks, cutting as it does directly into an assailant's angle of attack.

To throw the attacking lead leg side kick, place your rear leg directly behind your front leg. Bend the knee of your front leg, keeping the heel in line with the hip. Drive your lead leg forward with plenty of hip behind it, making contact with the heel. At the finish of the kick, the heel, knee, hip and shoulder should be in a straight line. (Figs. 50 and 51)

The defensive lead leg side kick is the stop/hit version of the kick, and is exactly the same as the attacking lead leg side kick, but without the initial step up. Practise this kick in both its versions on the bag and the focus pads. As with all stop/hit techniques, the 'snap up' focus pad drill should be used to practise timing. The main targets are the stomach, floating ribs, thigh, lower abdomen, knee, and the shin.

Fig 50

Fig 51

Spinning Backthrust Kick

This kick is widely thought to be the strongest of the kicks. Its power is derived from first using the strongest muscles in the leg to thrust and then by adding rotational power to that thrust.

The danger with this kick is that you must turn your back on your opponent and in a street situation this is potentially fatal, so timing is vital.

Fig 52

Throw the kick only:

1) When your assailant has been stopped in their tracks by a stop/hit.
2) When they are on the back foot, either mentally or physically.
3) As part of a combination.

To throw the kick, step across with your front foot until it is on the centre line of your stance. Spin, ensuring that your head, shoulders and hips precede the leg. Bend your knee and pick up your leg so that the heel faces the target. Continue to spin, driving the heel in a straight line. Make contact with the heel. (Figs. 52 to 55)

Fig 53

This is the kick in its most basic form. You should practise until you can eliminate stepping across to the centre line of the body as this will telegraph the kick unless you are careful to disguise it. Further, you can spin and throw the leg straight from the floor. This will reduce the kick's power, but is very deceptive.

Fig 54

The main targets for the spinning backthrust kick are the shin, knee, lower abdomen, thigh, stomach, liver, and kidneys.

Fig 55

Fig 56

Head-Butt

The head-butt is a close-range strike whose power is derived from its weight – the head weighs approximately 15 lb – and the hardness of the skull. It can be thrown in a front, rear, side or rising motion.

A particularly effective attack is to grab your assailant's head and drive your thumbs into their eyes. Then slam the top of your forehead on to their nose or the rim of their eye socket. (Fig. 56)

Strong neck muscles and quick reactions are essential to obtain the maximum effect from the strike. A neck muscle development programme will prevent self-injury and increase your striking power when using this technique.

It important to train on soft equipment such as a soft shield to prevent training injuries. Never be tempted to train on hard surfaces such as tightly-packed heavy bags – the *least* damage you will sustain will be concussion!

The targets for the head-butt on the head are the bridge of the nose, the cheek bones, orbit of the eye and the chin. On the body the targets are the solar plexus, stomach, and the small of the back.

Chapter Three
The Pre-emptive Strike

My dictionary defines a pre-emptive strike as: 'a strike intended to prevent attack by disabling a threatening enemy.' The words 'threatening enemy' have special importance here for legal reasons. If, because of another person's behaviour or language, you feel physically threatened, then you have the right to strike first. When someone's behaviour or words threaten you, a crime has been committed; a *common assault* has taken place.

Example

You are driving along a road when suddenly the driver of the car behind you starts flashing his lights. You have done nothing wrong and decide to ignore it. The driver of the car behind continues to follow you, flashing his lights and sounding the horn. In the rear-view mirror you can see he is agitated.

Confused as to what the problem is, you pull over to the side of the road and get out, intending to apologise for whatever it is that you've done. The other driver pulls over. He is bigger than you. He approaches you swearing and shouting and then says, 'You stupid **** I'm going to smash your teeth in!' He clenches his fist and raises his hand.

He has committed a common assault and you are entitled to defend yourself by use of a pre-emptive strike!

The Three Ranges

The closer your potential assailant is, the more dangerous it is for you. The further away they are, the fewer are their options. This is never truer than when there is more than one potential assailant.

Close range is less than three feet.
Medium range is three to six feet.
Long range is more than six feet.

Logically, a weapon will increase your assailant's reach and account must be taken of this.

Close Range

Situation One: You are clearly threatened at close range. Grab his head with both hands and head-butt him on the nose. At the same time perform a rising knee kick to his groin. Push him away from you and leave the area. (Fig. 57)

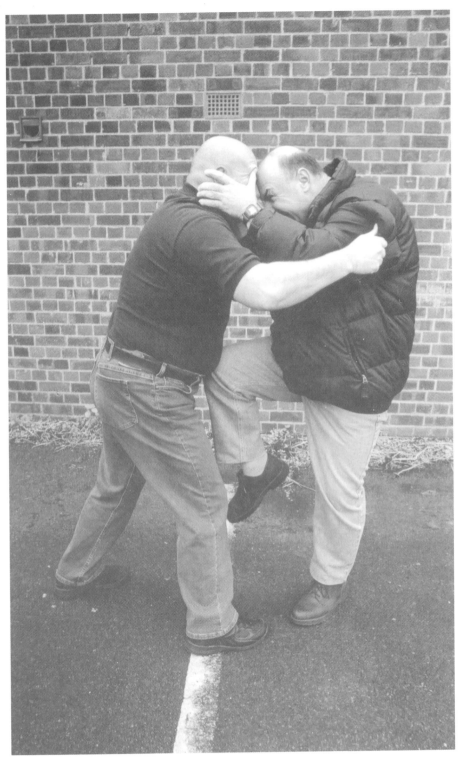

Fig 57

Medium Range

Situation Two: An argument becomes overheated and your potential assailant suddenly draws back his right arm in preparation for a right hook to your head. You perform a fast jab to the face. Grab him, spin him around and push him away. Leave the area immediately. (Figs. 58 to 60)

Fig 58

Fig 59

Fig 60

Fig 61

Medium Range

Situation Three: An aggressive beggar approaches you in the street. You try to sidestep him and continue on your way. At this point he threatens to hit you – the aggressive begging has just turned into a mugging. You throw a right cross to his chin and then immediately follow with a left hook. Leave the area immediately. (Figs. 61 to 62)

Fig 62

Medium Range

Situation Four: A man in a multi-storey carpark is harassing a woman. She is clearly frightened and looks towards you for help. You remonstrate with the man. He turns and comes towards you quickly. Throw a low defensive lead leg front kick to his lower abdomen as a stop/hit. Follow with a roundhouse elbow to the temple. Together with the woman, leave the area immediately. (Figs. 63 to 64)

Fig 63

Fig 64

Long Range

Situation Five: Whilst manoeuvring your car into a parking space it nudges another parked car, to which there is no obvious damage. A man appears from inside a nearby shop and starts swearing and shouting at you. You do your best to placate him, but he is very angry and takes a pace towards you, making it clear he is going to hit you. You throw a low roundhouse kick to his common peroneal nerve, re-cock your leg and throw a roundhouse knee kick to the same target. Leave the area immediately. (Figs. 65 and 66)

Fig 65

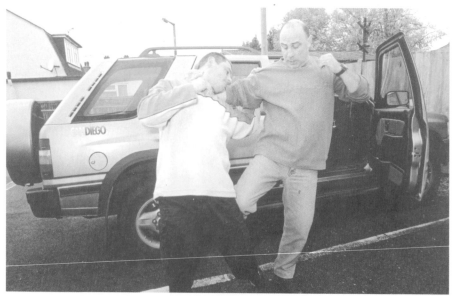

Fig 66

Summary

By defending yourself and then leaving the area, you have complied with the law. If you hang around to inflict further damage on your assailant it is *you* that has committed a crime.

However, if having defended yourself your assailant continues to attack you, you can continue your defence. Complicated? Yes. That is why it is essential for you to leave the area as soon as possible. It is important to tell the police that you were in fear of your safety and that your pre-emptive strike was as a result of the other person's threatening behaviour.

Chapter Four
Hold-Breaking

An observation of any fight will reveal that grappling is inevitable. Usually after a flurry of blows, the two antagonists will close and wrestle, either standing up or on the ground. It cannot be emphasised enough that grappling and hold-breaking skills are essential requirements for effective self-defence.

If you are attacked by more than one person it makes sense for one of them to get hold of you to (a) stop you from getting away, and (b) restrict your attempts to fight back.

Fig 67

Fig 68

Fig 69

Further, if you are held and your assailants have a weapon you are in very serious trouble. It is a relatively simple matter for them to grab you and stick a knife in your ribs. Equally, it is very difficult for you to defend yourself against a weapon whilst your movement is restricted.

Being held in a fight is a deadly serious business and no effort should be spared in breaking the hold at the first opportunity. When I first took up kick boxing, the rule systems of some organisations allowed throwing – Thai boxing still does. I managed to exploit this because judo was the first martial system I had trained in.

I quickly found it was a general truth that if someone wanted to stop you hitting them, they first had to grab and pin you, but this set them up for being thrown. Further, the act of grabbing set them up for being hit. Both throwing and hitting skills are needed in combat and the ability to flow smoothly from one skill into another is essential.

Further, in street situations I found that bigger, stronger men would try to rush and overwhelm me before I could hit them. Throwing skills that exploited their commitment of weight and movement were essential. I also learned that it was important to sidestep and hit an assailant from an angle. Standing in front of a bigger, stronger man and throwing punches was at best a gamble. It was not hitting them that was the problem, it was stopping them in their tracks before that superior weight and strength took effect.

It has to be said that the best time to break a hold is before it is on. Any attempt to grab you must be dealt with rapidly. No one merely holds you; they pull you onto a head-butt, punch or knee, push you against a wall or off balance, or else hold you steady and hit you. Therefore the instant your assailant reaches for you, slap their hands aside and hit them with a sharp combination – a head-butt followed by a right roundhouse to the thigh. (Figs. 67 to 69)

Fig 70

This area of self-defence spills over into pre-emptive strikes.

Single Lapel Grab

Situation One: A man grabs you by the lapel and pushes you backwards.

Go with his force and pivot strongly to your left.* Snap a fast jab to his chin. Now grab his wrist with your left hand and turn it so that his little finger is uppermost. Drive a descending elbow strike down onto his wrist. Drive a rising knee kick into his face. (Figs. 70 to 72)

Fig 71

*If possible it is better to yield to a push and take advantage of your assailant's strength rather than resist and be unbalanced.

Stay alert. Because they are down does not mean they are out. It is good practice to assume that your assailant is not alone. Quickly scan the area for further assailants and then leave the location.

Fig 72

Fig 73

Double Lapel Grab

Situation Two: A man grabs you by both lapels and pulls you forward.

The instant that you are grabbed, bring both your forearms down on your assailant's elbow joints, then simultaneously head-butt his face and knee him in the groin. Finish with a right roundhouse elbow to the jaw. (Figs. 73 and 74)

A forceful blow to the inside of the elbow joints will buckle them and makes the head-butt/knee combination fast, very powerful and almost impossible to avoid. The elbow finish is natural and flows nicely from the opening combination.

All three weapons employed, head-butt, knee, and elbow, are close-range weapons and particularly suited for hold-breaking.

Fig 74

Double Lapel Grab

Situation Three: A man grabs you by both lapels and pushes you backwards.

Go with his force and pivot strongly to your left. Execute a sleeve-pulling hip throw.★

Snap a roundhouse kick to the face as he lands.

★*Sleeve-Pulling Hip Throw (Figs. 75 to 77)*
Take hold of your assailant's arm at the elbow by the right sleeve. Take hold of his left arm underneath the elbow. Pull strongly with your left arm and drive upward with your right. Pivot to your left and bend your knees, placing your hips just below his hips. Continue pulling and pushing whilst straightening your knees quickly. Your assailant will go over your right hip.

The points of emphasis are:

1) A strong pull with the left hand.
2) A strong push upward with the right arm.
3) Bend your knees and place your hips below your assailant's hips.
4) Suddenly straighten your legs.

Once again the principle of yielding to force comes into play. This is one of the guiding principles of judo from which the sleeve-pulling hip throw is taken.

With a little practice this throw is very street adaptable and, executed quickly, it gets rid of your assailant almost before they have begun their attack.

Fig 75

Fig 76

Fig 77

Fig 78

Fig 79

Rear Arm Pin

Situation Four: You are grabbed from behind and lifted off the ground.

Snap a back head-butt into your assailant's face. Place your right hand behind you, grab his groin and twist. Break the hold by thrusting both your arms out to the side. Twist to your right and drive a rear elbow strike into his liver. Turn and throw a left hook to his jaw with plenty of follow-through. (Figs. 78 to 81)

The turning movement after the rear elbow strike to the liver should put maximum power in your left hook. Be sure to co-ordinate the turn with the punch and pivot your ankle, hip and shoulder behind it.

In any hold-breaking situation it is important to remain flexible. Double up on any or all strikes if necessary. Try to maximise your power by twisting your body behind each strike. This is of particular importance when you are attacked from the rear and accuracy is difficult.

Fig 80

Fig 81

Rear Choke

Situation Five: You are seized from behind with a rear choke.

From this position your assailant can crush your windpipe or render you unconscious. It is important to react very quickly and disable him.

Hold his elbow with your right hand and quickly turn your head into the angle of his arm, dropping your chin at the same time. This will relieve the pressure on your windpipe, but you are still in danger from the pressure on your carotid arteries. You now have only seconds in which to break the hold.

Drive a rear elbow strike into your assailant's solar plexus, then bite into his arm. Pull the arm away from your throat and turn out under the arm, forcing it up his back. Drive a rising knee strike into his coccyx, and push him forcefully away. (Figs. 82 to 84)

The knee strike to the coccyx is a very strong inhibitor in that once struck, your assailant will have problems moving effectively.

Fig 82

Fig 83

Fig 84

Fig 85

Rear Choke

Situation Six: You are seized from behind with a rear choke.

Stamp down hard on your assailant's foot, then step backwards with your right leg. Seize the arm around your throat and pull down. Throw your assailant with *ganseki otoshi*.★ Stamp down hard on his shin.

★Ganseki Otoshi (Figs. 85 to 89)
The name of this technique means 'to drop a big rock'. Seize your assailant's arm, driving backwards with your right leg, thus destroying his balance. Then pull his arm strongly forward and down whilst rotating your body to the left. Your assailant will be pitched forward and over onto his back.

The points of emphasis are:

1) Make the drive backwards with the right leg sudden.
2) The arm pull should be simultaneous with the backward leg movement and the pull should be maintained throughout the throw.
3) Rotate your body to the left as your assailant is pitched forward.

This particular throw is deceptive and very fast. Your assailant will be pitched over before he can react. Try not to be pulled to the ground with him when he goes over.

Your finishing kick should be fast and snappy and should connect the second he hits the ground.

Fig 86

Fig 87

Fig 88

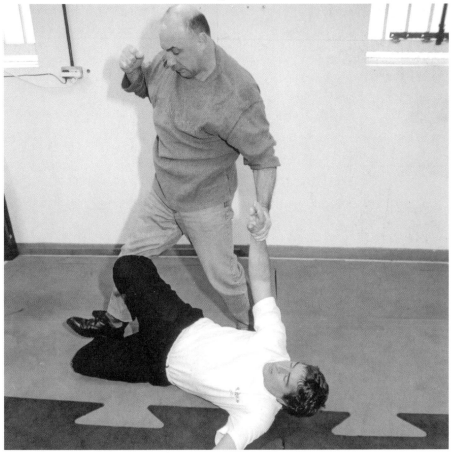

Fig 89

Head Lock

Situation Seven: Your opponent has seized your head and is exerting pressure on your neck.

This is a very dangerous situation. It is very easy for your assailant to strangle you, dislocate your neck or apply a thumb gouge to your eyes from this position. You must break the hold immediately.

Throw a left hook to his kidney. Reach up, grab his hair★ and tear it back violently. Throw a right hook to his chin, then finish him by driving a rising knee kick into the small of his back. (Figs. 90 to 94)

★If your assailant's hair is too short to grab, use his ear or hook your finger in his mouth and tear it backwards. Be careful not to fumble the mouth hook, you could have your finger bitten off!

Fig 90

Fig 91

Fig 92

Fig 93

Fig 94

Head Lock

Situation Eight: Your assailant has seized your head and is wrenching it painfully downwards and away from you. You are in danger of having your neck dislocated and must strike very fast to distract your assailant.

Tense your neck and drive a right hook into his groin. Throw him down with a *yoko guruma.*★ Drive a right descending elbow into his lower abdomen.

Regain your feet quickly and scan the immediate area for other assailants.

★Yoko Guruma (Figs. 95 to 98)
This technique is a 'side wheel'. It is from a range of judo techniques known as *yoko sutemi waza* – side sacrifice throws. As with all sacrifice throws, you hold your assailant tightly and then throw yourself to the floor, taking him with you. The landing is very heavy for the person being thrown and may, on a hard surface, see the end of the confrontation there and then.

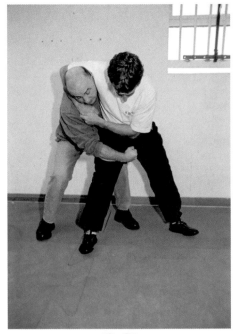

Fig 95

To throw him, grasp his left hip with your left hand. Place your right hand on his lower abdomen. Throw your right leg between his legs, pull strongly with your left hand and push upward with your right palm against his lower abdomen. As you fall, throw him over your left shoulder.

The main points of emphasis are:

1) Pull hard on his left hip.
2) Push strongly upward with your right hand.
3) Throw your right leg between his legs fast.
4) Commit totally to the technique.

Fig 96

I have used this technique and can vouch for its effectiveness, however, as all sacrifice techniques take you as well as your assailant to the floor, you must never use it in a gang-attack situation.

Remember to double up on all strikes whenever your assailant continues to fight back. This book offers advice and guidance, it is not a bible.

Fig 97

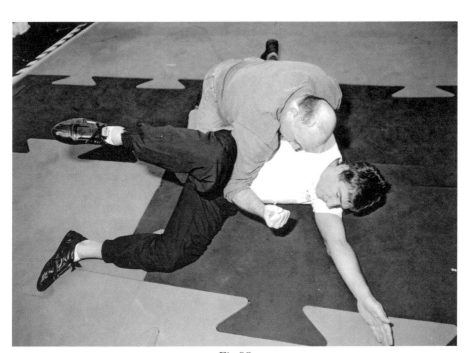

Fig 98

Standing Spine Lock

Situation Nine: Your assailant has grabbed you from behind and is applying pressure on your spine by pushing your head forward.

From here your assailant can break your neck. Death, or at the very least serious injury resulting in paralysis is likely if your neck is broken. You must act quickly and decisively.

Bring up both your arms and, using the backs of your hands, push against your forehead to counter the pressure on your neck. Drive your right heel down and smash it into your assailant's instep. Drive downwards with both elbows to break the grip. Spin and drive a left elbow strike to the side of his head. Throw him with a *tai guruma*.★ Finish with a roundhouse kick to his face.

★*Tai Guruma* (Figs. 99 to 104)
This technique is a 'body wheel' and works on the 'jack and roll' principle of throwing, a category into which approximately 50 per cent of throws fall. Technically it is quite simple to perform and is therefore particularly suitable for combat.

To execute the throw, place your left arm over your assailant's left shoulder, your right arm between his legs and bend your knees. Hold him tight and imagine a spindle running through both your bodies at navel height. Now lift with your legs and turn him around the imaginary spindle, throwing him forcibly onto his back.

Fig 99

Fig 100

Fig 101

The main points of the throw are:

1) Ensure you bend your knees enough.
2) Keep in mind the idea of a spindle running through you that you spin your assailant around.
3) Keep your assailant close to your body as you execute the throw.

As with all throws you can give him a more severe landing by pulling the throw short and allowing him to fall on his head. This turns the throw into its own finishing blow. However, the damage to your assailant is *considerable* and the legal consequences of any defence should always be borne in mind.

Fig 102

Fig 103

Fig 104

Rear Armlock

Situation Ten: Your assailant has grabbed and twisted your arm into your back.

As with any hold-break it is important to try to prevent your assailant getting the hold locked on before starting your defence.

The instant you feel your assailant exerting pressure on your arm, turn into a spinning elbow strike and hit him on the side of the jaw or on another suitable head target. (Fig. 105)

Be ready to follow with other strikes and kicks. Make sure to utilise your whole body in the rotation and put some real zap into your elbow strike. Practise this on a shield and feel the power.

If your assailant succeeds in locking your arm you must immediately tense that arm to prevent injury and pain. Drive a rear elbow strike to his temple as before and twist to your left, out of the lock. Now snap a lead leg front kick to his lower abdomen and finish with a right cross. (Figs. 106 to 108)

I have been on the receiving end of a rear armlock and once on, the hold is very hard to break (see the final part of this chapter). Act swiftly and break that hold.

Fig 105

Fig 106

Fig 107

Fig 108

Summary

The essentials of hold-breaking are:

1) Hit your assailant the *instant* you feel any attempt to grab you.
2) *Double up* on strikes, especially when grabbed from behind.
3) Curve your body behind the strikes to *maximise* power.
4) *Always* assume that your opponent is not alone and that *any* hold is potentially very dangerous.

Finally, just to make the point:

In 1966 I joined the army as a junior leader at a camp in North Shropshire. During my two and a half years there I joined the battalion judo club and after training hard, got into the judo team and went on to become team captain.

Unfortunately, when I was due to go into full service at eighteen, I had double surgical fractures of both legs just below the knees and was consequently held back while my friends went off to the depot. Some weeks after being discharged from hospital and only two weeks after coming off elbow crutches, I went into town for a drink with another soldier.

We had a few drinks, were neither drunk nor too loud and met a couple of girls who we agreed to walk home – innocent times! As we got outside the door of the pub, my friend, a small man, took off his jacket to put around the shoulders of one of the girls as it was cold. This innocuous gesture started an incident which is forever burnt into my soul.

One of the pub bouncers stepped forward and said, 'Who are you taking your jacket off to?'

Before my friend could reply he was grabbed and thrown against the plate glass of a shop on the other side of the alley to the pub. It was so off the wall that I just stood there. Fortunately the glass didn't break. At that point I called out to the bouncer to leave him alone. (I said I was innocent!)

The bouncer, around thirty, taller than me and twice as wide, responded by turning and throwing a right hook that, had it landed, would have done serious, and I mean serious, damage.

At that point training took over. Without thought – or sense – I sidestepped the right hook and performed a sweeping hip throw on him. He sailed through the air and landed with a satisfying thud, or at least it would have been satisfying had he stayed down.

Holding his shoulder, he got to his feet and rushed me in a crouch. Again, without thought, I performed a stomach throw on him (á la James Bond!) and again he hit the concrete with a truly impressive sound.

At this point in the story it might be worth considering that for James Bond the fight would have ended there and he would have gone someplace to make love to a woman of jaw-dropping beauty. Me? I was still in a fight that was about to get very nasty.

Although I had thrown him successfully with the stomach throw, the bouncer held on.

I got to my feet before him, but he spun onto his knees in front of me and took a tight grip on my collar, which he refused to release. I gave him several extremely good reasons to let go – a double knife-hand to the ribs, knee to his face and a roundhouse elbow of which I am still proud of today – but, and this really is the point of the story, he still wouldn't let go!

That's when the two other bouncers joined in. My arm was twisted up behind my back and I was punched and kicked from every angle. Unable to escape, frightened and angry, I bit, butted, spat, punched and kicked like a madman, but received more than I could give back.

The only thing in my favour was that none of the bouncers were very clever. They should have kicked my feet out from under me and stamped me into the deck. As it was I 'merely' got whacked from every angle. Perhaps it was the fierceness of my defence or the sobering sight of their friend on his knees. I later found out via the police that his collar bone had been broken.

There is another side to this story. I was aware of a gathering crowd of onlookers, some of them soldiers, lending advice, 'Give 'em a judo chop!' 'Oh good shot!' It even included some wry social commentary, 'Fuck 'is luck!' but no one helped me, not even the chap on whose behalf I'd intervened!

Somehow I broke free from the arm lock and stood before the bouncers. It was an uneasy and tense few seconds, but it looked like none of us wanted to carry on. Certainly they didn't seem in any hurry to resume and I was grateful just to be able to stand up.

They looked at their friend with the damaged shoulder groaning on the ground and then at each other and here, I kid you not, are the actual words used by one of them: 'You ought to be careful using that unarmed combat . . . you could kill someone!'

The next day I could barely move. I was covered in huge bruises, limped very painfully for a few days and my right arm was badly strained, but thankfully nothing more serious.

I took several lessons away with me that night, but the single most important one was never, ever, let someone get hold of you and if they do, break the grip as fast as you can.

Chapter Five
One-to-One – Unarmed

The title of this chapter is arbitrary. You should never take it for granted that your assailant is both alone and unarmed.

However in legal terms your defence must be lawful; that is, using minimum force only. It stands to reason that an attack by more than one assailant or by an armed assailant is inherently more life-threatening and the law *should* allow more extreme defences on your part.

So for that reason alone, the following scenarios involve one unarmed assailant only. You should be aware that your assailant may be considerably bigger than you, may be able to bench press 350 lb, may be mentally deranged or pumped full of drugs or drink, both of which will make him less responsive to pain.

Further, the situation may lend your assailant an unusual advantage. He may ambush you in the dark or attack you from behind. He may be a burglar, alert and full of adrenalin whilst you are bleary-eyed and half asleep. The scenarios where he has an inherent and potentially fight-winning advantage are too numerous to mention, but depend on one thing: if you are the victim he'll hold most of the aces.

There are in fact, so many potential extras to an 'unarmed assault' – drugs, drink, concealed weapons and so on – that the best advice I can give you is to treat all attacks as potentially life-threatening. However, observe the precautions of not jumping up and down on your assailant's unconscious form (!) and of leaving the area as quickly as possible. All attacks should be reported to the police.

Fig 109

Fig 110

Defences

Left Hook: Close Range
Situation One: Your assailant throws a left hook at your head.

1) Duck the attack and weave to the outside. (Fig. 109)
2) As you rise, drive a rising left knee into his lower abdomen.★ (Fig. 110)
3) Throw a hard right hook into his kidney. (Fig. 111)
4) Throw a left roundhouse elbow to his face. (Fig. 112)

★The act of ducking the left hook creates 'stored energy' in your bent legs, which dramatically increases the power of the rising knee strike. Practise bending and rising into the knee strike on a big bag until you are able to deliver real power.

Fig 111

Fig 112

Right Cross: Medium Range
Situation Two: Your assailant throws a right cross at your head.

1) Lean back and snap a lead leg front kick to his lower abdomen.* (Fig. 113)
2) Slam a hard roundhouse kick into his left thigh using your shin. (Fig. 114)
3) Throw a whipping right elbow to his temple. (Fig. 115)

Fig 113

*The snapping lead leg front kick counter to a right cross is a direct steal from sport kick boxing; only the target differs. This counter works because the leg is longer and stronger than the right cross. You should work the 'snap up' focus pads drill to make this technique sharp.

Fig 114

Fig 115

Fig 116

Fig 117

Right Hook: Medium Range
Situation Three: Your assailant throws a right hook at your head.
1) Slip the punch to the left. (Fig. 116)
2) Throw a right cross to his solar plexus or liver. (Fig. 117)
3) Throw a roundhouse kick to his neck using your shin.★ (Fig. 118)

★High kicks in self-defence situations are controversial. (See Chapter Two) The reasons that a high kick has been included here are:
1) The assailant has been weakened by a punch to the solar plexus.
2) An angular kick thrown from both outside and underneath the arm is hard for the assailant to read.
3) The roundhouse shin kick to the neck is a real man-stopper. This kick should be worked on the big bag religiously.

None of these reasons should distract you from the previous warnings that head kicks carry a high degree of risk.
   You should also note that a right hook is the most natural and powerful blow that an untrained assailant can throw. Usually it is easy to read, but do not underestimate its power and speed.

Fig 118

Groin Kick: Medium to Long Range
Situation Four: Your assailant throws
a groin kick.
1) Shuffle back and deflect the kick
   with a lower parry. (Fig. 119)
2) Slam a hard roundhouse kick into
   the thigh of his attacking leg using
   your shin. (Fig. 120)
3) Pivot strongly and throw a left hook
   to his jaw. (Fig. 121)

Fig 119

Because your assailant has been turned
by the lower parry, the left hook comes
out of nowhere and the angle makes
it a devastating shot.

In fact the whole combination is
simple, fast and very strong. It is a very
good example of why kick boxing has
so much to offer in the field of self-
defence. As a general note, it is
important to curve the body behind
your shots to maximise their power.
The difference in mechanical power
between 'arm only' shots and those
delivered with rotational power and
body weight behind them is
considerable.

Fig 120

Fig 121

Fig 122

Front Kick: Long Range
Situation Five: Your assailant throws a front kick at your body.

1) Sidestep to your left and deflect the kick with a right lower parry. (Fig. 122)
2) Throw a deep left roundhouse kick (a cutting kick) to his thigh, cutting his leg out from under him.★ (Fig. 123)
3) Throw a right roundhouse kick to his face. (Fig. 124)

★The cutting kick is one of the specialities of Thai boxing. It is thrown at the standing leg when your opponent has attempted to kick you and all his weight is borne by the support leg. It both 'cuts out' the support leg and damages it in the process.

Fig 123

Fig 124

Head-Butt: Close Range
Situation Six: Your assailant tries to head-butt you.

1) Twist to your left and drive a flat palm to his forehead. (Fig. 125)
2) Throw a short right cross to his chin without raising your elbow. (Fig. 126)
3) Pivot strongly over your left foot and throw a left shovel hook to his liver. (Fig. 127)

This defence requires fast reactions and an appreciation of what is likely at close range. You must be very wary of head-butts – they can finish you before you even know you are in a fight. Try to maintain distance and use a pre-emptive strike if you feel the situation has become threatening.

Fig 125

Fig 126

Fig 127

Fig 128

Fig 129

Summary

The attacks shown are simple and the most common. Together with the holds and hold-breaking methods shown in Chapter Four they reflect the most likely types of unarmed assault that you will encounter. However, cunning and improvisation are the lifeblood of the opportunist criminal and you must remain alert and flexible in your defence.

Never hesitate to double-up on your strikes if necessary. As stated before, on certain types of drugs, cocaine for example, your opponent may be nigh on invulnerable to your strikes. In such cases it is necessary to employ throws and strangles. It is outside the scope of this book to show the range and types of strangle/choking techniques in depth, but in terms of practicality I recommend the neck constriction. (Fig. 128)

To apply the constriction move to the rear of you assailant. Loop your arm around his neck so that his windpipe is in the crook of your arm. Use your other hand to tighten the hold. This constricts the carotid arteries and jugular veins in the side of the neck. It can take between half a second and ten seconds to knock someone out with this technique.

Warning: It is essential that you do not constrict your assailant's windpipe with your forearm as this may kill him!

You will be able to maintain better control if you can take him to the floor, but you should only do this when you are absolutely certain that he is alone. (Fig. 129)

If you are unable to leave the area as soon as you have completed your defence, move sharply out of range and to your assailant's side or rear. Never, ever, stand in his vision or range.

Chapter Six
Blunt Instrument Attacks

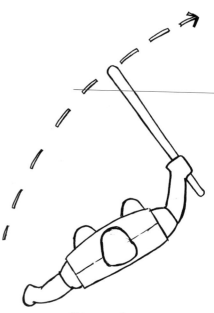

An armed assailant should be treated as a potential killer. An assault with a blunt instrument such as a cosh, baton, baseball bat or iron bar can render you dead or maimed with just one blow to the head.

Moreover, such weapons lend your assailant increased reach, leverage and frightening levels of power. Even if you successfully block such an attack with your arms, it may break your bones, thereby only delaying the outcome by one more blow of the weapon. (Diagram 4)

Diagram 4

Logic dictates that evasion – the movement of both the legs and upper body – is absolutely essential for you to stand any chance of victory when attacked with a blunt instrument. Movement can be backwards, to get outside of the furthest arc of the weapon; forwards, to move inside the arc of the weapon, or to either side, to give angular advantage.

The chances of you coming through unscathed in an encounter against a baseball bat-wielding assailant are slim. It may be necessary to take blows on the arms, shoulders and legs to protect more vital areas such as the head.

I personally know two individuals, one a weight-training karate black-belt and one a kick boxer, who had to fight off baseball bat attacks and got injured in the process.

The karateka cum weight-trainer took the force of the bat on his shoulder in a road-rage incident, then proceeded to beat the hell out of his assailant. The legacy however was months of treatment and physiotherapy to put the shoulder right.

The kick boxer, a British champion of genuine class and skill, blocked the bat but sustained a broken arm before going on to wipe the floor with his particular assailant!

Both of these men are good martial artists and their skill and bravery carried them through, but the cost in each case was very painful. I cannot emphasise enough that if you wish to defend yourself successfully, you must practise. Improvisation is all well and good, but skill, strength and speed are required when your back is against the wall.

From the second your assailant moves in to attack you should evade him by twisting, turning, ducking and rolling as well as by performing evasive footwork. Never, ever, stand still for a weapon attack. Your aim should be to minimise the strike's impact and accuracy even if you are hit.

Fig 130

Fig 131

Improvised defences such as crates, tyres, dustbins, cases and bags can be used as shields to deflect blows, and street furniture such as street lamps, obelisks and bollards can be used as obstacles or barriers.

It is vital to switch on and be very aware of the distance and timing factors. When he comes, he'll come quick and strong because he has all the advantages.

Should he try and play cagey by bluffing with the weapon and trying to force you off balance, you must immediately jam him and deliver a hard strike to his eyes, throat or groin.

Defences

Baton: Medium Range to Close Range
Situation One: Your assailant attacks you with an overhead strike.

1) Move in rapidly and jam the weapon arm with both hands as you head-butt your assailant's face. (Fig. 130)
2) Wrap up his weapon arm with your left hand. (Fig. 131)
3) Throw a tight right hook to the assailant's weapon arm.★ (Fig. 132)
4) Deliver a backhand strike with the baton against your assailant's thigh.★★ (Fig. 133)

Fig 132

★When you wrap up his arm, the baton should be tucked under your armpit and pressure exerted against your assailant's wrist so that when you hit his forearm with the right hook, it breaks his grip on the baton. Practise with a partner until you can do this quickly. It is a very effective disarming technique.

★★The thigh is a non-lethal target that may be struck hard. This will cause trauma to the large muscle mass and prevent your assailant continuing his attack. It will certainly prevent him outrunning you over a 100-metre dash.

Fig 133

Baton: Medium to Close Range
Situation Two: Your assailant attacks you with a forward diagonal downward strike.

1) Make a rapid sidestep to your left and throw a rear roundhouse kick★ to your assailant's groin. (Fig. 134)
2) Pivot and throw a left cross to his jaw or temple. (Fig. 135)
3) Pivot back and throw a tight right hook to his chin. (Fig. 136)

★The sidestep roundhouse kick to the groin is a very useful counter-attack in that the movement of the sidestep takes you out of harm's way whilst a back leg roundhouse kick to the groin is an extremely effective man-stopper.

I strongly recommend it against large unarmed assailants and almost any weapon attack. Practise it on the heavy bag until you can evade swiftly and deliver real power in the kick.

Fig 134

Fig 135

Fig 136

Fig 137

Baton: Medium to Close Range
Situation Three: Your assailant attacks you with a backhand strike.
1) Sidestep to the left and parry the attack with both hands. (Fig. 137)
2) Throw a right knee to the thigh. (Fig. 138)
3) Push down your assailant's arms with your left arm and pivot into a strong right roundhouse elbow to the throat.★ (Fig. 139)

★**Warning:** Blows to the throat are potentially lethal. Only you can judge the seriousness of the threat to your life.

Fig 138

Fig 139

Baseball Bat

The baseball bat seems to have become the street equaliser. Its reach and devastating impact make it a weapon of real terror. Some drug and terrorist gangs have added to its 'effectiveness' by hammering six-inch nails through it to create a modern-day mace.

With or without nails, a baseball bat is a fearsome weapon and should entitle you to use any means at your disposal in your defence. For practice, you should pad a three-foot length of broomstick, put on a head guard, elbow and forearm pads, groin protector and shin-guards, then have a friend try to hit you with the padded pole whilst you evade the blows. The difficulties of dealing with this weapon will then present themselves!

Never lose sight of the fact that one blow can end the fight.

Baseball Bat: Medium to Long Range
Situation Four: Your assailant throws a forward swing at your head.

1) Duck the attack. (Fig. 140)
2) Perform a right front kick to his lower abdomen. (Fig. 141)
3) Lever the head of the bat down and hook the handle end around his right wrist.★ (Fig. 142)
4) Drive the head of the bat into his face. (Fig. 143)

Fig 140   *Fig 141*

*This method of disarming is very effective and is extremely painful for the assailant. It is derived from an aikido technique called *nikkajo-osae***. It creates tremendous pain in your assailant's wrist and will enable you to prise the baseball bat from his grasp. Practise it until it is second nature.

**Nikkajo-Osae*
To perform this technique, drive the head of the bat down and then describe a small circle with the handle end, wrapping it around your assailant's wrist.

Push down on the handle end the second the wrist has been snared. This traps his wrist painfully and makes it possible for you to drive the head of the bat into his face. (Diagram 5)

Diagram 5

Fig 142

Fig 143

Baseball Bat: Long Range
Situation Five: Your assailant throws a downward strike at your knee.

1) Move back rapidly out of range and raise your leg to avoid the strike. (Fig. 144)
2) Move in quickly and push your assailant off balance at the arm and shoulder. (Fig. 145)
3) Turn into a right spinning elbow strike to the head. (Fig. 146)
4) Hook his right ankle with your right foot and sweep him. (Fig. 147)
5) Stamp down hard on his calf. (Fig. 148)

Fig 144

The sweep disrupts his balance and the stamp on the calf is both non-lethal and totally incapacitating. It will buy you time to leave the scene. All kicks to the leg have these twin advantages and, should the case go to court, you could point to your deliberate targeting of a non-lethal area.

Fig 145

Fig 146

Fig 147

Fig 148

Summary

Never underestimate the seriousness of weapon attacks. Leave the scene if you can. If forced to fight, assume that your life is in danger and react accordingly.

Use defensive movements to prevent accurate distance gauging by your assailant and take a glancing blow rather than a full strike. You must be fast and explosive in your counter-attacks to stand any chance of success.

If you get him in trouble, keep him there. Lastly, never fight a man with a weapon if you have any chance of avoiding it: pride mends more swiftly than bones – if you get the chance to heal.

Chapter Seven
Knife Attacks

There can be few areas of self-defence that are as laden with controversy as knife defence. A knife lends an assailant a courage and ruthlessness that ordinarily he would not possess, for it gives him the power to strike you down with one thrust or to wound you grievously with a slashing cut.

Further, most people attacked with a knife do not realise that a knife was used until *after* the attack, mistaking stabs for blows or in the case of cuts, not even being aware that they were there until shock has set in.

The availability of knives and the ease of their concealment makes them one of the most frequently used street weapons, and training in self-defence must take account of this. Whatever your skill level, you must never underestimate the danger of confronting a knife. For the purposes of self-defence any weapon capable of cutting or stabbing – broken bottles, screwdrivers, cut-throat razors and so on – should be dealt with in the same way as a knife.

Science and the Knife

During the Second World War, W. E. Fairbairn, a former assistant commissioner with the Shanghai Police, wanted to create an effective method of using the knife for the Commandos.

He started by going to see a famous surgeon and asking him for his advice on the most damaging way for a knife or dagger to be employed. What emerged became known as the Timetable of Death and the statistics contained within it make fascinating, if macabre, reading. They should give you pause for thought when considering the potential danger of a knife attack.

Timetable of Death

Artery	Size	Depth – Below surface	Loss of Consciousness	Death
Brachial	M	½ inch	14 Seconds	1½ minutes
Radial	S	¼ inch	30 Seconds	2 minutes
Carotid	L	1½ inches	5 Seconds	12 Seconds
Subclavian	L	2½ inches	2 Seconds	3 ½ Seconds
Heart	——	3½ inches	Instantaneous	3 Seconds
Aorta	——	5 inches	Depends on depth of cut	

The brachial and radial arteries are located on the inside edge of the upper and lower arms respectively. The carotid artery is found in the neck adjacent to the windpipe. The aorta is the main artery in the body that runs down the centre line of the torso.

Warning: Read and re-read the Timetable of Death. It should make you reconsider the wisdom of ever fighting a knife-wielding assailant – if you have the choice.

Fig 149

Fig 150

Fig 151

If you are attacked you will undoubtedly try to defend yourself. Therefore you must begin at the beginning, by developing fast, strong and effective techniques and then instilling, through hard repetitive practice, devastating counters.

Protection and Diversion

There is a range of tactics which, when employed, may assist you in your defence against a knife. Below are some of them:

1) If possible, you should wrap a jacket, shirt or scarf around your arm to prevent getting cut when you parry. (Fig. 149)
2) Use a chair. Turn it diagonally, pointing one of the chair legs at your assailant's throat and one at his groin, then rush him backwards against a wall or solid object and drive the legs into him. (Fig. 150)
3) Throw a handful of coins, dirt or stones into his face. Throw them as if you are throwing a knife. Step towards him and hurl them hard, about six inches away from his face. Kick him in the groin and run.
4) Use a length of stick, a bicycle pump, briefcase or shoes to attack his weapon arm at the wrist and deflect the blade. (Fig. 151)
5) Never forget that the eyes rule the world in which we live. Take them and your assailant becomes helpless!

The Five Essentials

1) **Body Evasion:** Twisting, turning, ducking and sidestepping should be used to avoid the point and edge of the knife and also to prevent your assailant accurately measuring the distance between you. Remain in constant motion throughout the attack and never confront your assailant head on – gain an angle and you gain a chance.

2) **Vital Points:** Go for vital points, particularly the four primary ones: eyes, throat, groin and the knee/shin area. Strike fast and accurately, and once you have your assailant in trouble, keep him there.

Fig 152

3) **Weapon Arm:** The weapon-bearing arm must be attacked and controlled.

4) **Attitude:** You must strive to win at all costs.

5) **Simplicity:** Keep all your defences simple and drive home the attacks.

Defences

Thrust to stomach: Medium to Long Range

Situation One: Your assailant thrusts to your stomach with the knife whilst using his front arm to guard against it being grabbed.

1) Sidestep to the left and throw a rear roundhouse kick to the groin. (Fig. 152)
2) Seize the weapon arm and spin under it. (Fig. 153)
3) Drive the knife into the body.★ (Fig. 154)

Fig 153

★The seriousness of this defensive counter should be obvious.

Never assume that a knife-wielding assailant will hold out the knife in front of him for you to kick or will be so stupid as to let you grab his arm easily. This defence shows only one of the ways in

Fig 154

Fig 155

Fig 156

which your assailant can make the knife difficult for you reach.

My friend and fellow martial artist, guru Jak Othman, master in seven styles of silat, has ways of concealing and using the knife that are simply frightening. Your assailant may have only one trick, but you can bet that he'll be a master of it.

Lapel Seizure and Thrust to Body: Close Range

Situation Two: Your assailant has surprised you and seized your collar.

1) Twist sharply to your right and parry the thrust with your right palm. (Fig. 155)
2) Throw a left hook to his throat. (Fig. 156)
3) Drive a hard side elbow into his ribs. (Fig. 157)
4) Slam a deep penetrating rear roundhouse into the back of his legs and cut them out from under him.★ (Fig. 158)

★Maintain your hold on his weapon arm throughout the defence.

Being grabbed and stabbed is a straightforward, simple and deadly attack frequently employed in street situations. You must react instantly and with maximum ferocity. When you have downed him, finish him quickly.

Fig 157

Fig 158

Backhand Slash: Medium Range
Situation Three: Your assailant
throws a backhand slash at your neck.
1) Move in quickly and parry the
   attack at the elbow and wrist.
   (Fig. 159)
2) Throw a hard front kick to his
   lower abdomen. (Fig. 160)
3) Hold the elbow firmly and snap
   down on the wrist, twisting the
   blade back across his face.★
   (Fig. 161. Also see Diagram 6.)

★The elbow snap and twist is very
effective and turns your assailant's
weapon back on him. Practise this
disarm until it is second nature.

Fig 159

Fig 160

Diagram 6

Fig 161

Fig 162

Fig 163

Overhand Stab:
Medium to Long Range

Situation Four: Your assailant runs at you and stabs downward at your chest.★

1) Step back and twist sideways. (Fig. 162)
2) Throw a lead leg side kick into his stomach. (Fig. 163)
3) Pivot and throw a left front kick to his groin. (Fig. 164)
4) Slam a rear roundhouse kick into his thigh. (Fig. 165)

★A running attack is very dangerous and hard for the defender to time. The use of the side kick stops him in his tracks and buys you a split second in which to throw heavier kicks that finish him.

Fig 164

Fig 165

Switching Hands Thrust:
Medium to Long Range
Situation Five: Your assailant suddenly switches hands and lunges at you.★
1) Sidestep to the right and block his attack with both hands. Seize and lock out the weapon-bearing hand. (Fig. 166)
2) Slam a rear roundhouse kick into his thigh. (Fig. 167)
3) Quickly follow up with a roundhouse knee into the same thigh. (Fig. 168)
4) Snap down his wrist and at the same time drive upward under his elbow with a bent arm and break his elbow joint. (Fig. 169)

★Switching hands is only one of the various tactics that your assailant may employ to fool you. The initiative lies with him because of the instinctive fear that a knife attack arouses. You must act rapidly and decisively if you are to stand any chance of defending yourself.

Fig 166

Fig 167

Fig 168

Fig 169

Summary

Defending yourself against a knife is a very risky business. The chances are that you will get cut and if the man attacking you is skilled in any of the knife based arts – silat or escrima for example – your chances are virtually nil.

If you are attacked you will, instinctively, try and protect yourself. With that in mind, go back and re-read 'Protection and Diversion'. As a rule of thumb, it is better to shout at or agitate a knifeman and calm a gunman.

Whatever happens, don't be a passive victim. If you shout, struggle or delay, your assailant may be forced to break off the attack. Deny him time and you increase your chances. The five essentials give you a chance, no more. Learn them by heart.

The Timetable of Death is quite simply a surgeon's bleak assessment of the potential damage caused by a knife attack. It should be read to reinforce the extreme dangers of confronting a knifeman.

Finally, to hammer home the theme of this chapter, here is a sobering, and at first hard to credit story of trials conducted by police in America.

Disturbed by the number of armed policemen being injured or killed, a policeman called Tulleners carried out a series of experiments where a knifeman was pitted against a pistol-carrying policeman.

Standing alongside each other the policeman and the knifeman were given tasks. The armed policeman's task was to draw his pistol, aim, fire and hit the target. The knifeman's task was to draw his knife, charge down the range and strike the target.

At all ranges under twenty-one feet the knifeman won, not just once, but every time.

Now mark out twenty-one feet and imagine you have a gun. It is almost impossible to concede that the knifeman has the advantage, but Tulleners proved it!

In this country it has only been in recent years that our police have been given the equipment – Kevlar vests, side-handle batons, CS gas – to deal with knife-wielding criminals, and then only because of a series of incidents where policemen and women were badly injured or killed. The clamour for better protection for the police was such that the Home Office and police authorities had to act.

You will not of course have the weapons the police are now armed with, and for you the situation would be all the more serious.

Lastly, should the point need to be driven home any more (pun intended), consider this. Many Special Forces personnel still carry knives into combat in theatres of war where every conceivable weapon, including short-barrelled automatic weapons made specifically for close combat, is available. They know, the police know, the criminals know: knives are deadly – perhaps the ultimate close-quarter weapon.

Chapter Eight
Gang Attacks

The greatest danger from a gang attack is being rushed and overwhelmed before you can mount a successful defence. So great is the danger of this that you must practise specifically to avoid it.

Further, if they get you down on the ground, and the odds are clearly in their favour for this, then you risk being severely injured or even killed. Keep on your feet and you double your chances.

Time is what they will try to deny you; time to strike back, to manoeuvre, to escape. Therefore you have to make time, you have to find ways of making them come at you one, or at the very least two, at a time.

If you want a clearer picture of the process by which a gang will attack, then just watch any of the natural history programmes that feature wolves, lions, hyenas, or cape hunting dogs.

A general scenario will go something like this. One attacker will confront you and draw your attention. Others will move to the sides and rear, while still others will close off potential escape routes. The instant you are engaged by anyone from the gang, the others will swarm all over you. You will be dragged to the ground and stomped into the pavement.

The more attackers, the greater the threat. Time, the angles of attack, 360-degree vision, strength and weight are all factors on their side. A strong, fast kick boxer who thinks quickly and acts decisively might be able to deal with up to three attackers. Beyond that you are in very dangerous waters and only a combination of courage, skill, strength and luck will get you through.

The moment you feel that a gang attack is likely, you must survey the area for an escape route. If escape is not possible then you must use whatever is in the area as a means of making them come at you in ways you can deal with.

Never let them come at you all at once!

In military terms anything that forces the enemy through narrow or confined gaps is called a defile. Look to make them move through defiles. If humanly possible, pick the ground on which to confront them. This factor alone may be the most important in surviving a gang attack.

The top of a staircase makes it very difficult for a gang to come at you from any angle other than the front. It also

Fig 170

Fig 171

Fig 172

makes kicking very difficult for them and places their heads close to your own feet. (Fig. 170)

A doorway also controls the angles. Logically, if there is anyway you can lock or bar the door, then do so. If not, then position yourself two feet back from the doorframe so that you can deal with attacks from the front, whilst denying your attackers the chance to launch assaults from the flanks. (Fig. 171)

They will counter this by rushing through the gap at you and by sheer weight of numbers force you backward into a more vulnerable position. Aggression and ruthlessness are the key. Strike hard at the first attackers, show no weakness and plant doubt in their minds.

In the street, crowd control barriers, the edges of walls, parked vehicles, shop porches, and lampposts restrict their angles of attack. Indoors, furniture, fixtures and fittings can serve the same purpose. (Fig. 172)

Lastly, if all else fails, place your back against a wall, thereby forcing them to come at you where you can see them. (Fig. 173)

Fig 173

Just because you keep the wall behind you doesn't mean you can't move. Twist, turn, bob, weave, duck and sidestep left and right. In short, do not become a static target.

Fine, I can hear you saying, but what if I'm out in the open, in a street or a deserted carpark? Well the answer is that you must use footwork to keep them all in your **line of sight.** (Diagram 7)

Aggression and ruthlessness are vital. Do not wait for them to start. Move in rapidly and hit as hard and fast as you can. Keep moving. Kick their legs out from under them and stamp on anyone that goes down.

Push or turn them into each other. If possible, after hurting one, lock him around the neck and use him as a shield. (Fig. 174)

If hurt, try not to show it as this will encourage them. Shout, scream, yell, or roar. Look, sound and act like the predator not the prey!

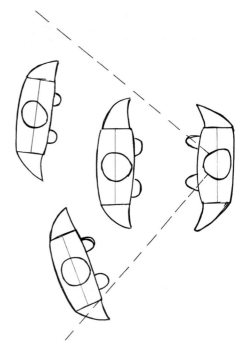

Diagram 7

Fig 174

Fig 175

Fig 176

Fig 177

One Against Two

Situation One: You are grabbed from behind and attacked from the front.

1) Beat the first attacker to the punch with a lead leg front kick to the stomach. (Fig. 175)
2) Follow up with a roundhouse kick to the thigh and down him. (Fig. 176)
3) Slam your head backwards into the face of the second attacker. (Fig. 177)
4) Drive your right leg backwards and throw the second attacker down with *ganseki otoshi*.* (Fig. 178)

Now leave the scene quickly.

*See figures 85 to 89.

The importance of hold-breaking was heavily emphasised in Chapter Four and the advice given then is applicable here. *Ganseki otoshi* becomes a devastating finisher when you drive your assailant head-first into the deck rather than pitching him on to his back.

Fig 178

One Against Two

Situation Two: You are attacked from both sides. One attacker is armed with a knife.

1) Block the punch of the first attacker with your left arm. (Fig. 179)
2) Throw a roundhouse elbow to his jaw and a knee to his groin simultaneously. (Fig. 180)
3) Turn the first attacker and push him into the second attacker. (Fig. 181)
4) Slam a roundhouse kick into the thigh of the second attacker. (Fig. 182)

Now leave the scene quickly.

I have mentioned using one attacker as a shield against another before. In this case you are not only using him as a shield, but also as a blind – the roundhouse to the thigh is almost impossible for the second attacker to see, let alone block.

Fig 179

Fig 180

Fig 181

Fig 182

Fig 183

Fig 184

Fig 185

Fig 186

One Against Three

Situation Three: You are attacked from both sides and the rear. One of your assailants has a baseball bat.

1) As the first attacker throws a left hook at your head, duck and shift to your right,★ throwing a combination of left shovel hook to his groin and a left hook to his throat. (Figs. 183 and 184)
2) Grab and push the first attacker into the second attacker with the baseball bat. (Fig. 185)
3) Throw a front kick to the knee of the third attacker. (Fig. 186)

Leave the scene immediately.

★The body shift has enabled you to see all three attackers and has placed you at an angular advantage to the first attacker.

The sequence above paints a very clinical picture. It may, in reality, require several heavy blows on your part to damage any assailant, so it is vital to keep moving, twisting and ducking and using your attackers as shields and blinds. To re-emphasise: think, act and sound like the predator, not the prey.

Attitude and aggression may win the day when everything else fails.

One Against Four

Situation Four: You are surrounded on all sides by four assailants. Two are armed, one with a knife and one with a baseball bat.

1) The first attacker throws a kick to your groin. Counter by sidestepping to the left, lower parry with your right arm and throw a roundhouse kick to his groin. (Fig. 187)

Fig 187

2) Push the first attacker into the attacker carrying the baseball bat. (Fig. 188)

3) Throw a side kick to the stomach of the second attacker as he attacks with a knife. (Fig. 189)

4) The third attacker makes a grab for you with both hands. Slap down his hands and throw a head-butt/right knee to the groin combination. (Fig. 190)

Fig 188

5) Throw a right cross to the throat of the attacker with the baseball bat. (Fig. 191)

It cannot be emphasised enough that you must move quickly and decisively. Keep twisting and turning and get them all in your **line of sight**.

The greater the number of assailants, the greater the danger, if for no other reason than time – time to hit them and time to move. If attack is inevitable then be in first. Strike as hard and fast as you can and be ruthless. Any other attitude will see you dragged to the ground and stamped on.

Fig 189

If you are downed, get up! Even if you suffer blows as a result, in a gang attack going down is the greatest danger. People talk of courage in fighting. Believe me, fear, ruthlessness and the desire to win are more important. Courage is so often another's perception of what he sees, not what the victim feels.

Fig 190

Fig 191

Summary

The best advice for gang attacks is to run away – if you can. If forced to fight, try and choose the ground. Force your attackers to come at you one at a time. Use natural and man-made obstacles to achieve this. Never stand still – move, twist, duck and turn. If you have to take a few hits in order to secure an escape route, then do so.

When fighting back use all your knowledge and skill. Be aggressive and ruthless.

Strike first and strike hard. Keep your feet at all times and if downed, get up fast.

Chapter Nine
Seated Defence

There are any number of situations where you might be attacked whilst seated. The first thing to note is the restriction on mobility. Some movement of the top half of the body may be possible, but if you are also hemmed in, such as in a restaurant corner or booth, or whilst seated in a car, you may have to conduct your defence from where you are.

One of the decisions that you will face is whether to try and stand or to conduct you first defensive actions whilst seated, bearing in mind that you may not get a choice.

If what you are sitting on – a railway seat for example – is stable and the attack is sudden, then brace yourself against the seat back and kick your assailant's legs. To try and stand is to immediately place yourself off balance and you will be pushed over and stamped on.

Conversely, if what you are seated on is potentially unstable – a free-standing chair for instance – then you will have no choice but to stand. (Read the incident at the end of this chapter.)

It is worth carrying out a few drills whilst seated, so see Chapter Eleven.

Car

Situation One: You are in the driver's seat and wearing a seat belt. As you stop at the traffic lights someone pulls open the passenger-side door and gets in.

Your assailant grabs you around the neck.
1) Drive a hard left elbow to his solar plexus. (Fig. 192)
2) Twist and throw a right hook to his chin or throat. (Fig. 193)
3) Grab his head with both hands and slam it into the dashboard. (Fig. 194)
Now push him out of the car and leave the scene fast.

This is an increasingly popular way of carrying out a mugging and is thwarted by the simple precaution of keeping all but the driver's door locked when driving in town. Good habits prevent situations from occurring.

Car situations are potentially very dangerous because you are restricted by the seat, dashboard and seat belt.

Taxi drivers are particularly vulnerable to attack and for them the situation is made worse because the attacker is behind them. The answer to this situation is to have a barrier between you and the passenger compartment and to be able to lock the rear seats from the front. Then if they try anything you can drive them to the nearest police station.

The most vulnerable time for a taxi driver is when taking payment. Open your window only sufficiently to accept the fare. Never place your arm outside your vehicle.

Unfortunately many minicabs do not have screens or lockable rear doors so the next defence deals with a situation in this type of car. If you are attacked in this way the odds are very much in the mugger's favour. It may be better to give the mugger the money and depart with your life.

Fig 192

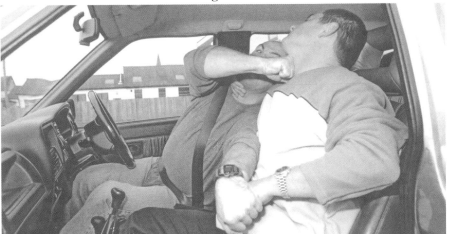

Fig 193

Fig 194

Car

Situation Two: You are in the driver's seat and wearing a seat belt. The car is stationary. Your assailant is in the rear seat and has placed a knife against your throat.

1) With both hands push the knife away and downwards. (Fig. 195)
2) Drive your left elbow into his weapon arm, forwards into the biceps and down onto the mid-point between the biceps and the triceps. (Fig. 196)
3) Twist and drive your left elbow into his throat or face. (Fig. 197)
4) Bite into his weapon hand and make him release the knife. (Fig. 198)

Fig 195

Fig 196

It cannot be emphasised enough that if it is only money that your assailant is after then give it to him! If you suspect his aim is to wound or kill you – the attrition rate of taxi drivers is a sad fact of modern life – then you will be forced to fight back. It is wise to plan your potential responses in advance – it may give you an edge.

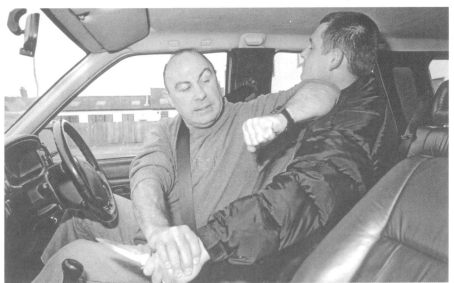

Fig 197

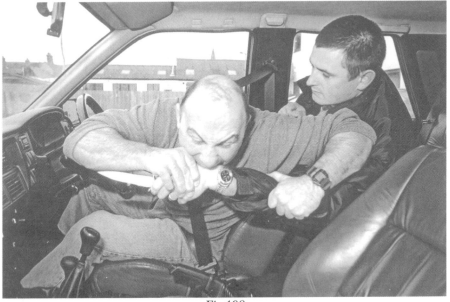

Fig 198

Restaurant

Situation Three: You are sitting in a restaurant when two assailants attack. One has armed himself with a knife from his table. You are hemmed in and have little room for manoeuvre.

1) Push the table towards them to create a barrier. (Fig. 199)
2) Come around the side of the table and slam your right knee into the first assailant's thigh. (Fig. 200)
3) Push him into the second armed assailant. (Fig. 201)
4) Throw a right cross to the second assailant. (Fig. 202)
5) Drive a descending elbow between the shoulder blades of the first attacker. (Fig. 203)
6) Leave the restaurant immediately.

Fig 199

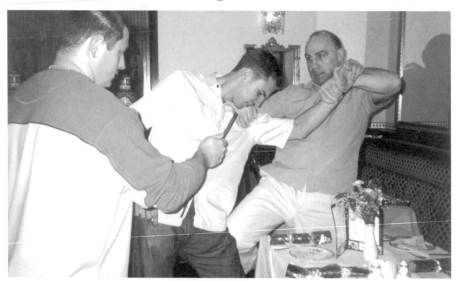

Fig 200

Restaurant situations are always dangerous because of the number of potential weapons available to assailants – knives, wine bottles, glasses and chairs – and the limited room to manoeuvre. Do not expect other people to help you; in my experience the best you can expect is for someone to call an ambulance after it is all over.

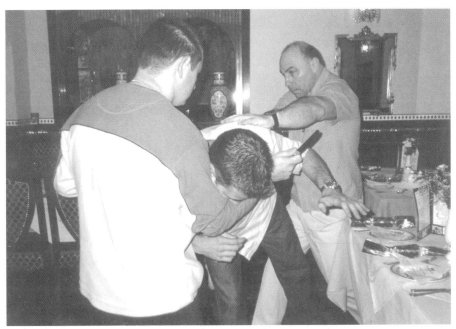

Fig 201

Fig 202

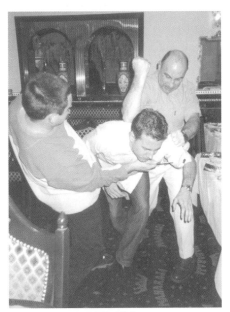

Fig 203

Park Bench

Situation Four: An armed mugger attempts to rob you.
1) Throw your book into his face to distract him. (Fig. 204)
2) Snap a front kick to his lower abdomen. (Fig. 205)
3) Stand and throw a right cross/left hook combination. (Figs. 206 and 207)

Fig 204

Fig 205

Note that the first part of this defence starts whilst you are still sitting. Attempting to stand without distracting your assailant leaves you vulnerable.

The action of throwing the book into his face will distract or blind him temporarily, gaining you the split second needed to drive home the front kick. Standing up whilst he is distracted enables you to launch a finishing combination with real power behind it.

Fig 206

Fig 207

Summary

All these scenarios are idealised. You should stay flexible in your responses and strike hard and fast when the opportunity presents itself. Once you have gained an advantage, keep it.

Decide whether to start your defence seated or standing. Be aware of your environment and seek to make it work for you. Beware of the instinct to try and stand up immediately; you are at your most vulnerable at this time.

Many years ago I became involved in an incident that came out of nowhere. So unexpected was the encounter that I acted without thought and managed to save a friend from serious injury or death. Looking back, I realise the seriousness not only of the attack, but also of my response.

One evening some friends and I went for a drink after work. We had a few and then split up. One of my friends and I planned to carry on the evening, but decided to get something to eat first. We went into a restaurant and were seated at a table by a young waitress who was chatty and friendly. My friend placed his jacket over the back of the chair next to him. It was early evening and there was no one else in the restaurant.

The waitress took our order and went into the kitchen. Immediately we heard the sounds of raised voices. Suddenly an irate man came out of the kitchen and started shouting at us. Bemused, my friend and I looked at each other. The man insisted that we change tables.

We had been placed at this table by the waitress, there was no one else in the place and no 'reserved' sign on our table. We hesitated and the man picked up my friend's jacket and threw it across the restaurant to another table. My friend got to his feet and words were exchanged, but my friend didn't swear, shout or wave his arms about, he simply asked what the hell was going on.

The man suddenly launched himself at my friend and threw two quick punches. One landed and my friend pushed the man away and shouted at him to stop. Up until this point I had done and said nothing. However, as the man went backwards, he turned and picked up a glass and tried to break it on the edge of the table. My friend was hemmed in between the table and the wall and had nowhere to go.

Had the fight remained a fist fight I would not have intervened, but the minute the man went for the glass I judged the situation as very serious and potentially fatal.

I came off the chair I was sitting on and in one motion brought the chair over my head and hit the man across the head twice. The chair broke and he fell, but as we tried to leave, he grabbed my friend's leg. (Hold-breaking rears its head again.) I kicked the man's hand away, pulled him to his feet, hit him in the stomach, spun him and sank two more shots in his kidneys. This all sounds very professional, but it was fast and scrappy.

We fell against a rail alongside a stairwell and the man tried to choke me. I hit him and turned him over the rail straight down the stairwell. At this point the kitchen staff exploded into the dining part of the restaurant and my friend and I made a run for it.

To this day I have no idea what was going through the attacker's head. Maybe he was the jealous type, but what took place between the waitress and ourselves was light, harmless and non-sexual in nature. Maybe they'd had a row before we arrived, maybe he was obsessive about her, but nothing we did or said was offensive by any definition.

A potentially fatal attack erupted from nothing and was compounded by the environment – my friend was hemmed in for most of the confrontation – and our failure to appreciate the seriousness of the encounter from the outset.

I do not recommend the use of weapons in defending yourself, but this whole incident was so fast and so potentially deadly that I had no choice. I used what was to hand and I believe I did not use more than minimum force.

Chapter Ten
Ground Defence

As discussed in previous chapters, losing your feet in a street situation is potentially disastrous. All your opponent has to do is jump on your head and the fight is over. If you are knocked to the ground, get up immediately, even if you have to take a few blows in the process.

In the event that you are downed and forced to fight from the floor, you must strive to keep your feet between you and your attacker, pivot to maintain position and kick out at your attacker's shins, calves, knees, thighs or groin.

Keep your elbows tucked into your sides to protect your ribs and your hands either side of your head. Lie on your side with your most powerful leg uppermost and drive a hard side kick into your assailant's shin as he moves in. (Fig. 208)

Roll and get to your feet as quickly as possible.

Fig 208

On the Ground

Situation One: You have been pushed over and have landed on your back. Your assailant has moved to the side and is about to deliver a head kick.

1) Pivot and throw a hard low roundhouse kick into his calf.★ (Fig. 209)
2) Roll backwards and get to your feet, ensuring that you keep a tight guard with your hands as you do so. (Fig. 210)

★It is important to 'go through' the target (his lower leg) with as much speed and power as you can and knock his leg out from under him. Once you have gained your feet, slam a roundhouse into his thigh to prevent him continuing his attack.

Fig 209

Fig 210

Situation Two: Your assailant has kicked your leg out from under you.

1) As you fall, turn towards your assailant. (Fig. 211)
2) Drive a hard roundhouse kick into his groin using the ball of your foot. (Fig. 212)

With practice this counter works well and at the very least stops your opponent closing in the second you are down.

The sequence is simple and should sound in your head like a mantra: **kick, get up, disable him and run.**

Fig 211

Fig 212

Fig 213

Situation Three: Your assailant has forced you to the ground and is about to finish you with a stomp.

1) Roll into him and grab his support leg. (Fig. 213)
2) Drive your elbow into the back of his knee joint and bring him to the ground. (Fig. 214)

This counter requires speed and commitment. It takes a hard elbow blow to buckle his knee, but when you achieve it he drops like a sack. Practise on a heavy bag until you can deliver it with real power.

Fig 214

Summary

If you go down, get up as fast as you can. If forced to fight from the ground remember the sequence: kick, get up, disable him and run.

There are a number of things that you should practise for use in situations where you are forced to fight back from the ground:

1) Pivot so that your legs are between you and your assailant.
2) Keep your elbows tucked in and use your hands to protect your head.
3) Kick heavily into your assailant's shins, calves, knees, thighs or groin.

Remember that it is better to take a few blows and struggle to your feet than to attempt to defend yourself from the ground – harsh, but true.

Chapter Eleven
Environment –The Unknown Factor

In the ring there are few variations in the conditions. The ring may vary in size and the surface is occasionally more slippery than normal, but basically that's it.

In combat the conditions under which you may be forced to defend yourself are potentially endless and a grasp of the problems posed by those conditions may save your life. Below are some of the more common variations that will affect fighting conditions.

1) Ground: Smooth, uneven or steep ground can affect kicking and fast movement.

2) Footing: Wet, icy, or muddy surfaces, gravel, crumbling earth or unstable sand can affect balance, kicking and even basic movement.

3) Light: Day, night, dawn or dusk. In poor light you may be forced to fight in close. In good light you may be conspicuous.

4) Clothing: Weather conditions will affect the type of clothing you and your opponent might wear.

(a) Winter: Long heavy clothing affects target choice. Hitting the body and groin is unlikely to be accurate or effective. It may also affect what techniques you can throw as movement may be restricted.

(b) Summer: Light clothing brings a whole range of targets on-line, both on yourself and on your assailant and can open out the potential technical response options.

(c) Protective Clothing: Motorcyclists are virtually armoured! Your technique and target choice will be limited against someone fully-clad in leathers and helmet. (Fig. 215)

Security personnel, including doormen, have unfortunately been known to cause rather than stop incidents. (See Chapter Four.) Be advised that such people may well be

Fig 215

wearing groin and shin guards, Kevlar vests and in unregulated establishments, have a whole range of concealed weapons, from electric stun guns to knuckledusters.

In a recent incident I heard about, the doormen took someone into a first-aid room, held him down and bashed the hell out of him. His crime? Being drunk and lippy. We live in interesting times.

All this may sound like I am prejudiced against doormen. Nothing could be further from the truth; I know a good number of doormen and the majority do a difficult job well, but the job sometimes attracts the wrong sort and vetting procedures aren't always what they should be.

5) Confinement and Dimension: The techniques you can throw in a car are wildly different from those you can throw in a carpark.

(a) Lifts, telephone boxes, dining booths, cars, train compartments and toilets are common areas where confinement may affect your options and prevent your escape. (Fig. 216)

(b) Staircases, corridors and subways also restrict your escape options and are potential ambush areas. (Fig. 217)

(c) Open areas such as carparks, fields and streets allow you to be attacked from all sides simultaneously, but grant you room to manoeuvre.

Opportunist criminals such as muggers are well aware of these factors and seek to use them whenever possible. It is important to make choices about how and where you travel and to know which suspect areas to avoid.

Fig 216

Fig 217

The Senses

Theoretically this heading could be included under Chapter One – Awareness, but is included here because of its bearing on environmental factors.

Hearing

Hearing works best when there is no background noise – sneaking up on someone in a nightclub is easy! The reverse is obviously true. When walking down a road late at night sounds appear magnified because they are isolated. Noise does not have to be loud to alert you; in fact, noise in the wrong location will switch you on faster than anything else.

Small noises may give away the fact that you are being followed or that someone is lurking nearby, but we can talk ourselves out of this awareness for fear of overreacting. This is the logical part of your brain overruling deeper, more primitive survival responses. Trust your primitive side; it's been around longer.

If you believe you have heard something then try half-opening your mouth and turning your head from side to side. This helps you pick up on small sounds and home in on their location.

Sight

The eye is constructed to pick up shape, colour and movement. In good light all parts of the eye work together to give the brain the fullest possible picture to interpret. In bad light, colour recognition is greatly reduced if not eliminated. In bad light you should look slightly off centre because the outside of the eye detects movement. It gives rise to the phrase 'I saw it out of the corner of my eye.'

Sensory Awareness

I know of no other name by which you can describe the sensations that alert you when the other senses don't play a part. That sensory awareness exists is open to debate, but you should consider the evidence of your own experience. Have you ever entered a building and known immediately that someone was there? Or perhaps you've entered a building and been utterly sure that you are alone. How? How do you know? What process is brought to bear to give you this information?

We explain away these sensations as 'feeling uneasy' or 'just knowing'. Clearly something is occurring, and probably something very old that is built into our survival mechanisms.

Another name for sensory awareness might be 'tuning in'.

You can become so aware of a particular environment that you immediately detect the slightest changes. Nowhere is this more apparent than in our own homes and no clearer demonstration can there be than a mother waking from a dead sleep because her baby in the next room has stirred.

Hearing alone does not explain her arousal. She has tuned in, in fact evolution has tuned her in, and she is programmed to act for her baby's survival. Individual sensory awareness has been extended to include the weakest pack member.

When we take hearing, sight and sensory awareness together they add up to potent defence mechanisms. By living in cities and overwhelming our senses with the myriad distractions of modern-day life, we have distanced ourselves from our primitive defences. Primitive in that they were our first protection, not our worst.

If we were to live in the wilderness once again, we would find our five senses becoming more acute and our sensory awareness becoming fine-tuned. If they did not respond in this way we would be killed and eaten very quickly.

Summary

If we take on board the lessons of Chapter One – Awareness and this chapter, Environment, we may well avoid having to defend ourselves at all. Tuning in is not easy, but in any circumstances where you begin to feel uneasy, trust it! Change your route, switch on, look, act and sound confident.

Finally, a case where the so-called higher brain overruled instinct and I learnt a valuable lesson.

Many years ago I attended a kick boxing tournament in a potentially dangerous area of London which had been the scene of serious riots not long before. To give you some idea of how the area was viewed, both the local police and fire stations had – and still do have – heavy and highly visible security precautions.

Being a serving fire-fighter, I parked in the fire station yard and walked to the leisure centre where the kick boxing was taking place. The kick boxing finished late so instead of taking the longer route back via the main road I told myself that there was nothing to fear except shadows and an overactive imagination. So I took the shortest route, which was along a pitch-dark thoroughfare strewn with rubble.

I was alone, escape options were few and anyone lying in wait could have heard me coming a long way off. It was the perfect ambush site. This dawned on me about halfway down the thoroughfare, which was perhaps two hundred and fifty yards long. I started to switch on and had every sense screaming for information. Sweat broke out on my forehead and I cursed my stupidity.

In the event nothing happened, but my actions were plain stupid. For the sake of a few minutes extra travelling time I broke every safety rule there is. People have done less and been killed. I almost deserved to be attacked.

The first law of survival is avoiding the avoidable.

Chapter Twelve
Train for the Game

Compared to training for the ring, training for the street is difficult. As the preceding chapters have illustrated, there are few, if any, constants. What follows cannot be exhaustive, but should at least take you some way towards realistic training for combat.

If your line of work throws up recurring scenarios such as dealing with people over a counter or face to face, then give consideration to defending yourself in these circumstances first. You should also experiment and practise so you can handle specific situations where you are dealing with money directly with the public, especially if you are a shopkeeper, taxi driver or petrol station attendant; people who frequently face harassment or attack.

Analyse and adapt in the light of what you discover about your own strengths and weaknesses. Do not treat these exercises like a game. In order to have value they must be worked to the extent that you are under pressure and breathing hard.

When you have worked these drills to the limit, then extend their duration and intensity. Push yourself and remember the maxim of the Red Army: 'Train hard, fight easy!'

Multi-Directional Pad Work
Drill One
Stand with one assistant to your front with focus pads and one to your rear with a kick shield. Set the stopwatch for one minute and for the duration respond as quickly and powerfully as you can to your assistants' calls asking for a technique or combination of techniques. (Fig. 218)

Throughout the drill your assistants should move around, requiring you to change direction and range constantly. As you become more skilled your assistants should call out more demanding instructions. Finally, work up to four assistants.

Do not hold back: hit the pads and shields as though your life depends on it.

Fig 218

Drill Two

Experiment with Drill One in a variety of environments, some examples of which are given below:

1) On a staircase. (Fig. 219)
2) In a lift lobby.
3) Seated and ground defence scenarios.

In each case have the pad/shield holders move around and force you into tight corners where manoeuvring is difficult. This is very different from a smooth-floored, open and well-lit gymnasium and gives a taste of reality.

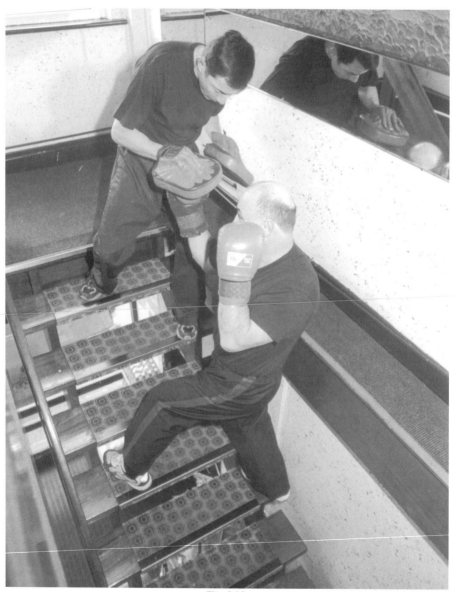

Fig 219

Drill Three

Pad up and go into the ring for some full-contact training. Wear a gumshield, groin guard, 16 oz gloves, shin/instep protection and perhaps body armour. (Fig. 220)

1) Practise kicks and punches above the waist and boot-to-boot sweeping to begin.
2) Next add leg kicks.
3) Add knees and elbows.
4) Finally add throws.

Warning: If you are not already a practising kick boxer you are about to go through a steep learning curve. Full-contact training is not for the faint-hearted.

If you are not used to full-contact training then have someone in the ring with you and your opponent to act as a controller to prevent things from getting out of hand. It is a common reaction for people not used to getting hit to get a little 'heavy' once they get cracked on the nose!

Start slowly and over a period of weeks build up the power in line with the control. Sparring of this sort is the lifeblood of kick boxing and is one of the most powerful reasons for recommending it for self-defence.

Fig 220

Drill Four

Spar against two or more attackers. Even if you are a kick boxer the problems of defending from two or more sides will test the best of you. Work with constant motion in mind – hit, move, grab, turn and sweep. (Fig. 221)

As in Drill Three, start with punches, kicks above the waist and boot-to-boot sweeping. Gradually add the extra elements – leg kicks, elbows, knees and throws as your ability to cope increases.

Once again, things can easily get out of hand so have someone to monitor the action and control it if necessary.

Fig 221

Drill Five

This is the same as Drill Three, but one of the attackers has a padded stick about the same length as a baseball bat. Have him attack your head, body and legs as you shorten and extend the distance between you to rob him of room and leverage. (Fig. 222)

Obviously, any training drill cannot replicate the fear and extreme danger of real combat, but imagination and intensity will provide many of the skills required if sufficient time is given over to them.

Fig 222

Drill Six

Similar to Drill Three, but you wear an old white T-shirt, industrial protective goggles and are padded up for contact sparring. Your opponent has a red felt-tip pen and is padded up for kick boxing sparring. (Fig. 223)

For two rounds of one minute you must defend yourself whilst trying to avoid both the punches and kicks of your opponent *and* the felt-tip pen. This is a sobering experience for anyone under any delusions about the dangers of facing a knife.

Over the two minutes you will invariably be hit and at the finish will be lucky not to be covered in red strike marks. Remember, a man with a knife does not have to strike hard, he merely has to run the blade across you – just like a felt-tip.

The extreme importance of taking your assailant out of the game fast will be brought home in a very obvious way.

Fig 223

Drill Seven

Ground Defence. Pad up for sparring and lie on the ground in the centre of the ring. Have two opponents pad up and for a two-minute round try and regain your feet whilst they attack you. (Fig. 224)

Get to your feet fast and try to keep them in your **line of sight**. At all costs do not allow them to grab you or position themselves on either side of you. This is an exhausting experience. Try two rounds of two minutes to begin with. Now try the drill again with three opponents!

Fig 224

Summary

Safety and reality are the two key opposing issues that have to be resolved when training. Too much safety negates reality and logically, too much reality negates safety.

Further, no training can generate the fear, pain and sheer ferocity of an actual assault, but with the right attitude, the drills above will work the skills that you will need to survive. Experiment, work hard and learn.

Chapter Thirteen
The X-Factor

In the introduction I highlighted the fact that kick boxing involves hard conditioning work-outs that enhance strength, speed and stamina beyond those of most martial arts. This physical conditioning is the X-factor that gives you the edge over a street assailant. Always bear in mind that drugs, drink, weapons and numbers are the street assailant's X-factors.

With so many factors in the street assailant's favour you must maximise your chances by attaining and maintaining a good level of all-round fitness. Only by keeping the sword sharp will you win.

In the first book in this series, *Kick Boxing – A Framework for Success*, I outlined the very strenuous physical requirements for fighting in the ring. The requirements to survive in the street are no less rigorous, but the emphasis is different.

A ring fight can last up to twelve rounds and therefore your stamina levels must be high, but a street situation may require an explosive burst of energy over in as little as twelve seconds. Equally, in extreme cases, it may last for ten to fifteen minutes of all-out sustained effort with the possibility of death or serious injury for the under-trained, the slow, the weak and the unfit.

Moreover, it has to be said that a champion in the ring is not always going to be a champion in the street. Approaching a street situation in the same way as the ring is potentially very dangerous. You will not be able to 'warm' your way into the fight or study videos of your opponent's previous fights.

You must switch on and stay switched on. Further, you must be explosive in your responses. The exercise routines outlined below will give you the means to stay sharp.

Strength and Power – The Hammer

The relationship between strength and power is frequently misunderstood. Strength is your potential to achieve a physical task. Power is applied strength: physical strength applied through technique.

Your ability to hit hard, to throw with force or to apply a grip whilst fighting is what concerns us here, that and nothing else.

Weight-training and body weight exercises will give you raw strength. Bag work, focus pads, shield work and throwing repetition (*uchi komi*) will give you power in technique. Weights and body-weight exercises are essential to give you the base that must then be worked through technique to achieve power.

Balance in training is of particular importance. If you overemphasise one aspect over another, such as too much strength training at the sacrifice of time spent on technique, you will be undermining your own efforts. Equally, too much time spent on developing speed at the expense of power will serve you badly when you need to stop someone quickly.

Strength
Weight and Resistance Training
In *Kick Boxing –A Framework for Success* I outlined a basic exercise routine that could be built on to take you into the ring. If you haven't read it I suggest you do so before reading on.

Here I will skip many of the basics and cut to the heart of what will give you explosive power and a good maintenance programme. I will only show an upper-body routine and explain later how to build up your legs through various running routines and bag work. This is not to denigrate weight-training routines for the legs, it merely reflects my own training and emphasis. Ultimately you may wish to embark on a full weight-training programme, but that is beyond the scope of this book.

In purely practical terms, I believe that a combination of weight-training and body-resistance exercises such as press-ups, affords the best maintenance programme for someone wishing to stay street sharp.

A number of years ago I was on the comeback trail after a long period away from ring fighting due to injury. A friend of mine, John King, was a weight-training instructor, as well as a 5th Dan in Go So kempo, a doorman with more than twenty-five years of experience, and a one-time kick boxer. He suggested that I come to him and he would coach me through a routine that would enable me to rip the heads off the opposition!

It was a routine devised to fit in with what was an already full training regime of running four times a week, sparring three times a week, bag work, skipping and pair and shadow-boxing three times a week.

With such a heavy training commitment it was important that the routine be of relatively short duration, but geared to provide maximum results. Also, because of the amount of running and bag kicking that I was doing, it was only an upper-body routine.

John's idea was to give me both anaerobic and aerobic training simultaneously. This was achieved by spacing out the workstations and making me run from one to the other between exercises to keep my heart rate up – which it did! He christened it the 'Killer Routine' – though I never got to the bottom of whether it was meant to kill the opposition or me.

Warning: If you are new to weight-training do not attempt this routine under any circumstances, especially the running between workstations. Build up to it slowly over a period of months. The best approach would be to do the exercises individually, as three sets only, until you can cope. Once you can deal with the exercises, place them back to back as described and then, only when ready, add the running.

This routine performed two or three times a week will give you a real edge and will enhance your ability to fight strongly.

Supersets – The Killer Routine

Supersets are exercises that work two opposing muscles groups in succession. I will explain and show the six exercises that will give maximum results in a short space of time and more importantly, provide a good maintenance programme.

The muscles that you need in punching are:

1) **Triceps:** Located at the back of the upper arm.
   These muscles straighten the arm and are therefore used in straight punching, the jab and the cross.
2) **The Biceps:** Located at the front of the upper arm.
   These muscles bend the arm and are therefore used in hooks and uppercuts.
3) **Lats:** Located down the side of the body.
   These muscles literally armour the body.
4) **Abdominals:** Located down the front of the body and extending from the sternum to below the navel.
   These muscles also act as armour against body shots and kicks.

Routine
Superset One

Dips (Figs. 225 and 226)
Curls (Figs. 227 and 228)
Perform 1 x 12 dips and then run to the curling station and perform 1 x 12 curls.
Repeat this superset three times.
Now run to the next workstation.

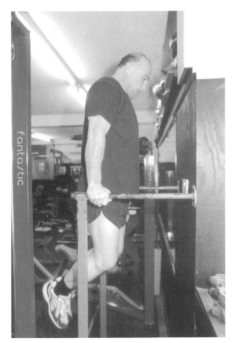

Fig 225   *Fig 226*

Fig 227

Fig 228

Superset Two

Wide Grip Chins (Figs. 229 and 230)
Upright Rowing (Figs. 231 and 232)
Perform 1 x 12 wide grip chins and
then run to the next workstation and
perform 1 x 12 upright rowing.
Repeat this superset three times.
Now run to the next workstation.

Fig 229

Fig 230

Fig 231

Fig 232

Superset Three

Inclined Sit-Ups (Fig. 233)
Leg Raises (Fig. 234)

Perform 1 x 25 inclined sit-ups and then run to the end of the gym and back. Now perform 1 x 25 leg raises.

Repeat this superset three times.

Fig 233

Fig 234

Summary

1) Practise each of these exercises individually until you reach a reasonable level of fitness.
2) Now change the routine by placing the exercises back-to-back and perform the supersets as described.
3) Link the supersets together into one holistic routine.
4) Finally, add the running between workstations.

Total time including running between workstations = 40 minutes.

There are any number of potential routines that give good upper-body strength, so if you have your own, fine, but as this whole routine can be done in 40 minutes, it has much to recommend it for someone heavily involved in skills-based sessions and running schedules.

Running

Once again, in *Kick Boxing – A Framework for Success,* I went into some detail as to the types of running that benefit a kick boxer and the schedules that will deliver the goods in the ring according to the duration you are training for – three, five, seven, nine or twelve rounds.

The task here is somewhat different. In the street you must go from zero to maximum performance in a split second without the benefit of a warm-up session. That calls for two basic requirements:

1) A good level of basic stamina fitness.
2) The ability to fight flat out from a dead start for five minutes.

To achieve a good basic level of stamina fitness you must jog or run 200 miles in 24 weeks.

This is achieved by running three times a week over increasing distances. Do not cut corners or reduce the 'base' schedule – the only person short-changed will be yourself. Further, to cut the base is to run the risk of injury. Build up slowly and surely.

The Base
1) 2 miles x 3 per week for 8 weeks = 48 miles
2) 3 miles x 3 per week for 6 weeks = 54 miles
3) 4 miles x 3 per week for 6 weeks = 72 miles
4) 5 miles x 3 per week for 4 weeks = 60 miles
Total = 234 miles in 24 weeks.

Also a word of advice on running in general. First get professional advice on a good pair of running shoes. Many of the running magazines do extended features on just what type of shoe you should be using. If necessary, write to one of them, tell them what you're training for and your mileage, and ask their advice. They exist for this purpose and they know their stuff. Secondly, run on grass. Heavy running on concrete roads has the potential to destroy your joints over a period of time.

Fartlek

Having put in the base and therefore achieved our basic stamina fitness, we now need to introduce the body to working anaerobically or without oxygen.

When you jog or run at low speed – eight to ten minutes per mile – your body is able to use the oxygen you're breathing to assist energy production. This is called aerobic (with oxygen) running. At faster speeds and when you are fighting flat out, your body will be working too fast to be able to use the oxygen and therefore you are forced to use different energy systems, otherwise you will go rapidly into oxygen debt, become winded, and will be unable to continue running or fighting.

In order to fight or run flat out, your training must take you into the anaerobic phase and to do this you need *fartlek*.

Fartlek is the Swedish word for 'speed-play' and was developed to combat the boredom and grind of athletes' running routines. Another name for it is varied speed running. It requires you to run some sections of your running session at a jog, some at a run and some at a sprint, hence varied speed or speed-play.

Formula

1) Run or jog half to three quarters of a mile as a warm-up.
2) Now jog for 100 yards, run for 100 yards and sprint for 100 yards, repeating this rhythm of jog/run/sprint for a mile and a half.
3) Finally, run another half mile at a jog as a warm-down.

This takes you into oxygen debt temporarily during the sprint phase and thus trains the body to fight or run flat out. If you have never done this type of running before you will feel it for a couple of days afterwards.

As you get fitter, you can extend the lengths of the varied-pace running, for example 200 yards jogging, 200 running and 200 sprinting. It is important to run at your maximum speed during the sprint phase.

Having first achieved the base, substitute two *fartlek* sessions for a run. This will also keep your training varied and interesting.

A maintenance schedule for someone who has put in the base now looks like this:

1) Monday jog 5 miles.
2) Wednesday run 2 ½ miles: ½ mile warm-up; 1 ½ miles *fartlek*; ½ mile warm-down.
3) Friday run 2 ½ miles: ½ mile warm-up; 1 ½ miles *fartlek*; ½ mile warm-down.

Hill Work and Step Routines

Running up and down hills and running up steps is a guaranteed way of building up your legs. The World Champion kick boxer Jean Yves Theriault had some of the strongest kicks in the sport and attained real man-stopping ability.

How he achieved this is interesting in that he turned a vice into a virtue. He found that the deep winter snow in his native Canada prevented his normal running routine, so he started running up and down the stepped tiers of the Ottawa Civic Sports Centre.

This involved running up a thousand steps at a time with the result that he put over two inches on his thighs and developed brutal, punishing kicks.

Hill work acts in the same way. The increased resistance of incline running will put your thighs under intense strain with the result that the muscles will gain power and size.

Find a stretch of hillside roughly a quarter of a mile long or a steep flight of stairs with at least a hundred steps. City tower blocks are ideal for this.

Perform a half mile warm-up run and then run a series of hill or stair relays with jog recoveries of say, one minute, between each climb. Logically, in the case of stairs, you walk down as fast as you can for your recovery period. Now perform a half mile warm-down jog.

These routines are killers to begin with, but the leg strength and size gain is considerable. It is important not to overdo the hill work and instead build it into a regular running schedule along with the *fartlek* and the long run.

Warning: There is always the temptation for beginners to overdo it. I can assure you that sustaining injuries is only a matter of time if you short-change the suggested schedules. Also, listen to you body. If you feel overly tired the day after exercising then reduce your schedule until you can cope.

Total Running Schedule

The total running schedule shown below should address all your needs with regard to leg strength, the ability to fight anaerobically and stamina maintenance.

1) Monday jog 5 miles.
2) Wednesday run 2 ½ miles: ½ mile warm-up; 1 ½ miles *fartlek*; ½ mile warm-down.
3) Friday run 2 ½ miles: ½ mile warm-up; 1 ½ mile hill work relays; ½ mile warm-down.

Power

Power is the technical application of force to the target. The aim of this section is to take the strength you have gained from the weight-training and the running and convert it into real hitting power.

Bag work is an essential component for converting strength into power. Whether it is kicking or punching that you are trying to develop, the rules are the same.

Select a technique or combination and throw ten repetitions into the bag as hard and as fast as you can – hold nothing back. Shake the limbs free and throw another ten. Shake the limbs free again and throw a third set.

This method should be used for all the techniques or combinations that you wish to build in power. You should aim to bury your shots into the bag; do not just strike at the surface. Also, your shots should accelerate, otherwise they become merely a push. A bag that is hit correctly will jump; a bag that is pushed will swing.

Power Maintenance Routine

Having built satisfactory levels of power, it is necessary to incorporate the power into an aerobic and anaerobic routine that works the heart, lungs and body in a technical work-out.

1) Perform three rounds of shadow-boxing as a warm-up.
2) Perform three rounds of two minutes duration with the hands only on the bag.
3) Perform three rounds of two minutes duration with the hands and legs on the bag.
4) Perform three rounds of shadow-boxing with weights in your hands.★

★Start with light weights of just one kg and slowly build to three kg. Do more if you can handle it, but increase the weight slowly and remember the aim is to deliver power, not become a body-builder.

This routine serves as a great builder of power and in conjunction with the total running schedule provides a solid maintenance programme.

Speed

A full breakdown of the elements of speed is given in Chapter Seven of *Kick Boxing – A Framework for Success* and it is strongly suggested that you read it. It deals with the isolation and training of the three component parts of speed:
1) Reflex speed: reactions
2) Limb speed: technique
3) Body speed: footwork

Here we are concerned with practice rather than theory and sports-based applications. We will only look at specific drills that will give you the basic requirements for the attainment and maintenance of speed.

Drill One

Number a series of simple combinations:
1) Jab/cross.
2) Jab/cross/left hook.
3) Jab/cross/rear roundhouse kick to the thigh.
4) Jab/duck/left roundhouse elbow/right whipping elbow.
5) Right cross/left hook/rear roundhouse to thigh/knee to thigh.

Now have someone move around you with focus pads calling out just the combination number. You must respond with the correct combination as fast as you can. (Fig. 235)

Fig 235

Drill Two

Put boxing gloves on. This drill has similarities to Drill One except that you have three people move around you; one with focus pads, one with a kick shield and one gloved up and wearing a head guard and gumshield. (Fig. 236)

The aim is for the focus pad and shield assistants to move around calling out combination numbers to which you respond while the third assistant throws simple combinations at you with reduced power. You must duck, slip, parry and block before delivering your own combination.

Fig 236

Drill Three

This is the same as Drill Two except no one calls combination numbers, they merely hold the focus pads or shield away from you and then suddenly snap them up so that you have to respond instinctively with the combination that comes to mind.

Drill Four

This is the same as Drill Two except that your assistants work closer in and you can only use your elbows, knees, head and low roundhouse kicks to the thigh.

Note that throughout these drills we have used combinations not single blows. You must not expect your first response to be up to the task and must be ready to launch another shot or combination to complete your defence.

For a complete breakdown of power and speed acquisition I suggest you study Chapter Seven in the first book in this series, *Kick Boxing – A Framework for Success*, which takes you through the nuts and bolts of this area of training.

Chapter Fourteen
Recommended Reading

The aim of this chapter is to recommend books that have worth and relevance to the subject of self-defence. Like a lot of long-term martial artists, over the years I have acquired a significant library of books that have assisted my development in one area of martial arts or another and some stand out from the pack as A-list manuals.

I have given each of these books a mini-review and a score out of ten. The choice is entirely subjective and of course you may disagree both with the book choices and my rating of them. Some of the books mentioned are now out of print, but between the library service and bookshops that carry out book searches, I'm sure you can track down copies if you are determined enough.

The A-List

1) *My Method of Self-Defence*
by M. Kawaishi
Published by **Foulsham**. Now out of print.

The author, Mikonosuke Kawaishi, was the technical director of the French Federation of Judo and this book, first brought out in the sixties, is a brilliant explanation of how judo techniques can be used for self-defence.

The techniques shown in the book do not conform to modern-day sport judo, but to the earlier methods of the kodokan that made great use of *atemi waza* (striking techniques), both to set your assailant up for a devastating throw, armlock or choke and to dispatch him immediately afterwards.

The defences shown are very practical and leave the reader in no doubt as to their effectiveness. As an ex-judoka I have often felt that judo is the great undiscovered fighting art and this book goes a long way to support that view.

Rightly, Kawaishi has given an entire section over to the knife. He shows a keen awareness of the danger of knife attacks and gives clear diagrams illustrating the places most likely to be attacked and the methods for dealing with an attacker.

The entire book is crammed full of solid advice on judo's combat applications and I have no hesitation in recommending it.
Rating: 7/10

2) *The Tao of Jeet Kune Do*
by Bruce Lee
Published by **Ohara**. Still in print.

This book is really a collection of Bruce Lee's notes and sketches, but clearly reveals Lee's unique fighting brain. An open advocate of cross-training and full-contact sparring, he epitomised the quest for reality in martial arts training. It is no surprise that he angered many traditionalists, especially in the Chinese community.

Nowadays the cross-training and the eclectic approach that he espoused is described as cutting edge, which gives you some idea of how far in advance he was of the rest of the field thirty years ago.

The techniques, ideas and explanations in this book inform, tantalise and reveal. Many techniques and combinations translate to either the kick boxing ring or the street with little or no adjustment. Page after page gives hard to find knowledge of the where, how, why and when of fighting: where to strike; how to deliver power; why range matters so much and timing, the art within the art. A 'must have' text.
Rating: 8/10

3) *The Filipino Martial Arts*
by Dan Inosanto

Published by **Know How**. Still in print.

Danny Inosanto could be described as the man who took up the baton when Bruce Lee died. He was also a cross-trainer long before the word entered the martial arts vocabulary. He built on Bruce Lee's ideas and then took his own direction, returning to his roots in the Filipino martial arts before branching out into Thai boxing, penjak silat and many other styles besides.

This book specifically outlines the Filipino side of his search and therefore contains information on unarmed combat and the combat use of the stick, knife and sword. It starts with the basic use of the stick and then goes on to show that the principles of both armed and unarmed fighting are the same.

By the end you are left in no doubt as to how deadly the Filipino arts are and the book should, if nothing else, give you pause for thought when considering facing an armed man.
Rating 7/10

4) *Dogs Don't Know Kung Fu*
by Jamie O'Keefe

Published by **New Breed**. Still in print.

Jamie O'Keefe, no relation but a friend, is a firm advocate of applied martial arts and has built a solid reputation as a consultant, teacher and researcher into the realistic options available to women, doormen and the man in the street. He has systematically stripped away the superfluous and dragged the theory under the spotlight.

His book, *Dogs Don't Know Kung Fu*, is primarily about women's self-protection, but much of what he has to say applies to men as well. He backs up his advice by quoting from real life instances where people have suffered heavily for being in the wrong place at the wrong time.

His words of caution about confronting a person on drugs and the description of the effect of those drugs on an attacker are backed up by his many years as a doorman where he has had to apply his hard-won knowledge.

Any of Jamie's books are worth having on your shelf, but if you have to choose just one, then make sure this is it.
Rating 8/10

5) *Black Medicine*
by N. Mashiro

Published by **Palladin**. Still in print.

This book is a detailed study of the vital points of the human body and demonstrates how to attack them. Such information can be found in many books, but the depth and clarity of *Black Medicine* make it stand out.

A combination of photographs and line drawings makes vital point location easy and the defences offered are simple no-nonsense answers to self-defence questions.

Whatever martial art you are involved in, from the point of view of combat the information in this text is indispensable.

Rating 8/10

6) *Bruce Lee's Fighting Method*
– Self-Defense Techniques
by Bruce Lee and M. Uyehara

Published by **Ohara**. Still in print.

After reading the *Tao of Jeet Kune Do,* then this book must be next on your shopping list. It has very little text, but the strength of the book lies in its easy to follow picture sequences. A range of defences is shown from armed to unarmed attack through to gang situations and seated scenarios.

Lee's own ability leaps off the page, but the defences are mainly simple and workable.

On a note of caution however, a number of high kicks are shown for defence and it has to be said again that the higher the kick, the greater the risk of being swept or rushed off your feet. For that reason only I must mark it down slightly.

Rating 7/10

7) *Black Medicine II – Weapons at Hand*
by N. Mashiro

Published by **Palladin**. Still in print.

This book follows on from the first *Black Medicine* and illustrates the use of both armed and unarmed methods to defend yourself. The armed defences utilise a great many improvised weapons and show ingenuity and not a little humour. As a companion work to *Black Medicine,* it is a solid buy.

Rating 7/10

8) *Dead or Alive*
by Geoff Thompson

Published by **Summersdale**. Still in print.

Geoff Thompson has become recognised as the United Kingdom's foremost expert in the field of applied martial arts. He has produced dozens of books on the subject of self-defence and has run seminars the length and breadth of the country. He has quite simply been on a crusade to force the martial arts community to confront reality.

In this book Geoff reveals the distilled wisdom of many years of experience and training. The subtitle of the book is *The Definitive Self-Protection Handbook* and that describes it perfectly. I will not waste time describing the contents in detail, but simply state that if you are serious about self-defence then go out and buy this book.

Rating 9/10

Appendix
Vital Points

Hitting the right point at the right angle with sufficient power and speed is the heart of effective self-defence. When your assailant is bigger, armed, or with others, then you have to be sure to land telling shots, and that means correct targeting.

The ability to land accurate shots under extreme pressure is perhaps the ultimate skill where self-defence is concerned.

Study the text of the book to familiarise yourself with the vital points. Then refer to these charts for more accurate descriptions. I would caution you to read the warnings that appear alongside the descriptions. The taking of a life carries very heavy penalties and should only be done in defence of your own life or that of another person.

Below is a series of illustrations and descriptions referring to the places to strike.

Vital Points: Front (Diagram 8)

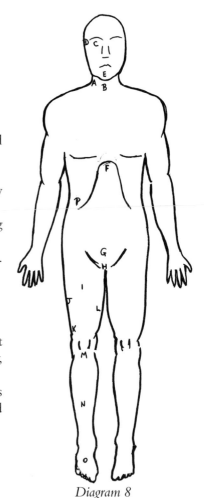

A) Carotid artery: Located either side of the throat. Knockout point.

B) Adam's apple (larynx): Warning: potential killer.

C) Eye: Can cause permanent damage. Use only in extremis.

D) Temple: Knockout point. Warning: potential killer.

E) Chin: Knockout point.

F) Solar plexus: Nerve conjunction just below the diaphragm. Knockout point.

G) Lower abdomen: Essentially you are hitting the bladder.

H) Testicles: Intense pain, will drop like a sack. Knockout point.

I) Front of thigh: Causes intense pain and muscle spasms.

J) Common peroneal nerve: Nerve running down the outside of the leg. This is a perfect self-defence target in that it hurts intensely, it immobilises and isn't lethal.

K) Muscle insertion point above the knee: This hits the nerve plexus just above the knee and produces the same results as hitting the common peroneal nerve.

L) Inside of thigh: Causes pain and muscle spasms.

Diagram 8

M) Kneecap: A snap front or side kick to the kneecap will drop him.

N) Shin: Perfect self-defence target, as the pain is intense, but will not kill.

O) Centre of foot: The bones are small and easily broken when stamped on. Also there is a nerve point located in the centre of the foot and stamping on this will incapacitate your assailant.

P) Liver: Located just under the lower ribcage on the right-hand side. The pain is intense and similar in severity to a kick to the groin. Knockout point.

Vital Points: Rear View (Diagram 9)

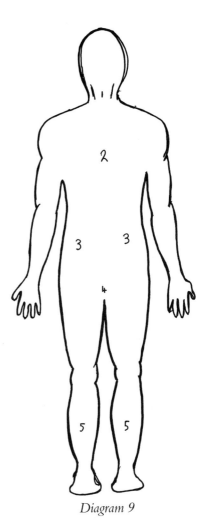

1) Nape of neck: Will cause whiplash and has potentially very dangerous results. Knockout point.

2) Mid-point between the shoulder blades: Will wind your assailant.

3) Kidneys: Will cause pain and nausea. A good weakener.

4) Coccyx: Base of the spine. Will incapacitate your assailant as all movement comes from the spine.

5) Base of calf muscle: Will cause intense muscle spasms and pain. A good target to unload on because it isn't lethal.

Diagram 9

Vital Points: Head (Diagram 10)

Warning: Any blow to the head can kill.

A) Carotid artery: Knockout point.
B) Adam's apple: Warning: potential killer.
C) Eye: Can cause permanent damage. Use only in extremis.
D) Between the eyes: Knockout point. Warning: potential killer.
E) Point of chin: Knockout point.
F) Temple: Knockout point. Warning: potential killer.
G) Occiput: Back of the head. Knockout point.
H) Hollow of throat: Warning: potential killer.
I) Jaw: From the angle of the jaw down to the chin. Knockout point.

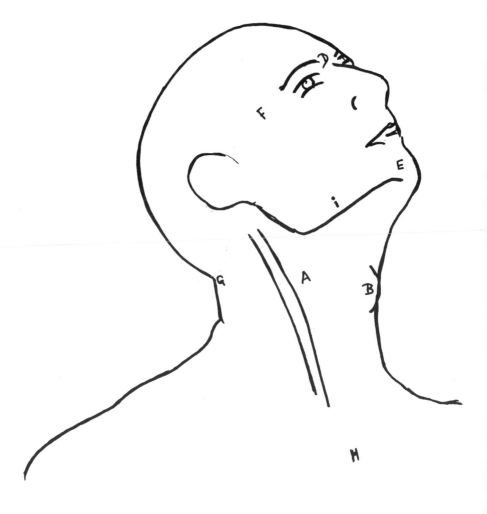

Diagram 10

By the same author:

Kick Boxing
Advanced Kick Boxing

www.summersdale.com